BRIGHTON

THE CENTURY IN PHOTOGRAPHS VOLUME II

CHRISTOPHER HORLOCK

S.B. Publications

DEDICATION

This second book is dedicated to my parents, Rhoda and George Horlock, still living at White Street, Brighton, where I was born. They took me to all the right places as a child – the Regent Cinema, the SS Brighton, the Hippodrome, the West Pier plus shows on the Palace Pier, at the Theatre Royal and Dome. All very formative!

First published in 2001 by S B Publications
19 Grove Road, Seaford
East Sussex BN25 1TP
01323 893498/fax 01323 893860
sales@sbpublications.swinternet.co.uk

© Christopher Horlock 2001

ISBN 1 85770 219 0

Typeset by JEM Editorial (jemedit@aol.com)
Printed by Tansleys The Printers
19 Broad Street, Seaford
East Sussex BN25 1LS
01323 891019

ACKNOWLEDGEMENTS

The majority of the photographs in this second book come from my own collection – but many people have again generously allowed pictures from their collections to be published, given copyright clearance or supplied specialist information for the captions.

In no special order, these are Robert Jeeves, Chairman of the Sussex Postcard Club, and proprietor of the Postcard Saloon, Branch 2, 36 Queen's Road, where all manner of collectable pictures and postcards can be bought; those two local history heavyweights, Trevor Povey of Shoreham and Bob Elliston of Eastbourne, both provided pictures and information; Peter Booth, Philippe Garner, Peter Bailey, Margaret Taylor and Janis Ede all loaned rare photographs and Brighton Reference Library supplied several views from its extensive archives, for which Stephanie Green, Picture Librarian, is to be thanked.

Many modern views were made available by Richard Taylor, picture editor of *The Argus* and feature writer Paul Holden. Bill Tulloch, Managing Director of architects, Fitzroy Robinson, gave permission for the 1960s Town Hall model to be reproduced and David Store, of Ordnance Survey, allowed the 1930 map to appear. Andrea Bishop of the National Motor Museum at Beaulieu, Adam Trimingham of *The Argus*, John Bidwell of Brighton and Hove Motor Club, Jasper South and Suzanne Mantell of Brighton and Hove Council and Carol Theobald all provided valuable information, with work colleague Martin Oborne again helping with computerisation.

Much of the copying work was undertaken by Tom Reeves of Lewes, whose care and attention at getting grading and sharpness just right, often from some pretty poor master material, is second to none.

Finally, I have to thank again, posthumously, the great veteran historian James Gray (1904-1998), who I visited for nearly twenty years at his Hove home. He told me virtually everything he knew about Brighton, both great and small, from when each and every street of council housing was built (fortunately I wrote it all down) to where an elephant is buried off the Lewes Road (it died while performing in a circus). His own unique collection of photographs is now safely housed with the Regency Society of Brighton and Hove. Another 'old timer', John Barrow of Hove (died 1991), gave me – literally – hundreds of old photographs he had hoarded while working as a freelance photographer and for the *Brighton and Hove Gazette and Herald*. When this paper folded and became the *Brighton and Hove Leader* in 1981, he scooped up hundreds more while a 'clear out' was taking place at the Argus offices and later passed them on to me.

They would be pleased that 'the great cause', as they both called documenting Brighton's history, goes on.

SOURCES AND REFERENCES

As before, newspapers have been the best sources of facts and figures when compiling the captions for this book. Period guidebooks were also useful, as were a large number of notes made by James Gray, passed on to me, following his death. Books included: *Life In Brighton*, by Clifford Musgrave (John Halliwell Publications, 1970); *Brighton Old And New*, by Antony Dale and James Gray (Batsford 1972);

Brighton Between The Wars, by James Gray (Batsford,1976); *A History Of Brighton General Hospital*, by Janet Gooch (Phillimore, 1980); *Brighton's Music Halls*, by David Adland (Baron Birch, 1994) and *The Encyclopaedia Of Brighton*, by Tim Carder (East Sussex County Libraries, 1990).

SPECIAL NOTES

One of the nicest aspects of doing a second volume of a book is being able to correct the mistakes in the first! The car park on the railway works site opened in January 1972, not 1971 (page 99), Churchill's last visit to Brighton was in 1961, not 1952 (page 92), and having gone through all the maps and directories again, I now make it eighteen streets and courtyards demolished for the Churchill Square development, not seventeen (page 113). Also, the town's first motorbus (page 46) was photographed either in 1903 or 1904, not 1902.

As with Volume I, distances and measurements are given in old imperial units. I'm sure anyone desperate for the metric equivalents will be able to work them out. Amounts of money are also given in old pounds, shillings and pence. Before metrication in 1971, twenty shillings made a pound and twelve pennies made a shilling, so ten shillings (written 10/-) would be 50p today, three shillings (3/-) would be 15p and so on. Two pounds and two shillings, written as £2/2/- (or £2/2/0) would be £2.10 today. There were 240 pence to a pound, so 120 pence made 10/-.

CH

CONTENTS

*Terminus Road in 1903, with horse cabs waiting to enter
Brighton Station – see page 49*

Introduction – Style and Sleaze,
Gems and Junk   5

The Early 1900s   8

World War One   52

The 1920s   56

The 1930s   66

World War Two   80

The 1940s and 1950s   85

The 1960s   97

The 1970s and 1980s   121

The 1990s   137

About the Author   144

STYLE AND SLEAZE, GEMS AND JUNK

This book supplements Volume I of *Brighton, The Century In Photographs*, but the area it covers is wider and spreads to the outskirts of the town to include Dyke Road, Lewes Road, the university at Falmer and areas of the Brighton bypass. Housing estates at Whitehawk, Moulsecoomb and Hollingbury are also included as are the racecourse and some of the town's old windmills.

But it's the seafront, piers and old town area that again form the main body of pictures. Here are the town's heart and soul and where changes somehow bring about the greatest feeling of loss.

Volume I generated a huge number of letters, 'phone calls and comments and the one I liked best was: 'No other book on Brighton that I've read gives such a desolate sense of old ways dying'. This was exactly the aim, as it's what I experienced myself growing up in the town during the late 1950s and 1960s. Born a year before rationing ended, even as a child I was aware of road widening, slum clearance and areas being irrevocably altered. I attended Saturday morning pictures at the old Astoria cinema in Gloucester Place, and would walk home with my brother through the enormous dereliction of the Richmond Street, Sussex Street and Carlton Hill area as it was at this time. We found brightly coloured, broken tiles among the rubble from the multitude of pubs that once proliferated in the area and even bonfires smouldering where very recent clearance work had taken place. Later, we saw Edward Street widened, Churchill Square being built, watched the last pantomime at the Hippodrome and the final film at the Regent. We had gone skating at the SS Brighton and saw ice shows there we still talk about. As teenagers we tried to act very grown up at the Top Rank Suite and new ice rink, but didn't really like either.

Crowds watch fishermen haul in a catch, 1905 – see page 11

Then the Brighton Centre was built and suddenly the seafront was thronged with people wearing conference badges and carrying attaché cases, instead of 'kiss me quick' hats and sticks of rock. Old ways were certainly dying and Brighton's post-war years were a watershed, where the town seemed to lose an awful lot and gain very little.

Those who say that Brighton isn't the town it used to be are right. No town or city stays fixed in time, but, to quote Winston Churchill: 'Nothing is wrong with change, as long as it's in the right direction.' The direction Brighton took after the war was the obvious one of becoming a conference town, with the seafront the focus for this, with its hotels and amusements already in place and the station not too far away. All the area needed was a state-of-the-art conference building, which it got in 1977.

But what people really mean by the town not being the same is the change in 'feel', atmosphere and sense of community, that's now so totally different from the inter-war years. Brighton today is undoubtedly an odd (and probably unique) mixture of style and sleaze, where a walk along the seafront will alternately dazzle with its views of sky and sea and the finest seafront architecture in the country, then utterly dismay, with cracked paving stones underfoot, black rubbish bags piled up in doorways and having to avoid drug addicts tottering into you or the aggressive appeals of beggars. The gems of Brighton perhaps shine all the more brightly because of the junk they contrast with so markedly.

Yet however concerned we are about the built environment that surrounds us, the slow erosion of many fine old buildings, large and small, seems to go on unabated, and Brighton is irrevocably taking on the appearance of everywhere else. Inside the new Churchill Square complex, seen near the end of the book, you could actually be anywhere – Bournemouth, Glasgow, even on the moon. Not one feature of its design acknowledges the history, ethos or nature of the town the building stands in. Not that the planners knew or cared anything about these anyway. Throw it up fast, build it cheap, with quality of design and blending with the surrounding environment low on the specification list. The 1980s Sainsbury's building, off the Lewes Road, at least echoed something of the old railway viaduct site it was built on, and new flats being built on Marine Parade in the summer of 2000 do have a stylish, deco look, which always seems to work for buildings on a seaside promenade. The restoration and enlarging of the Grand Hotel, following the bombing of 1987, was absolutely magnificent. They can do it when they want.

The book naturally concentrates on lost buildings and the changing topography of the town during the last 100 years. But, as in Volume I, the people in the pictures fascinate just as much as the buildings, streets and locations. All that was said before about people being changed by twentieth-century living applies again here. But an odd notion about people of the past seems to persist. Being much less sophisticated than we are now, it's supposed they were simple, trusting souls, easily pleased, who could be deceived fairly readily into accepting their lot in life and made to toe any line put out by those in authority. The people who populate these old photographs can't have known much, must have been very unworldly and happy to get by with few possessions, a modest bank-holiday now and again, and doffing a very respectful cap at their employers, the law and the general powers that be. Duty was an uppermost thought in their minds. Their own rights came a long way down the list of priorities, not that they had many anyway.

Today, we view these people with incredulity and know the 'good old days' depicted in old photographs was largely sham. No-one pulls the wool over our eyes; today we are enlightened, have control over what we say and do, with rights and legislation preventing us from being exploited. Well, maybe.

Taking a good number of steps back and looking hard at how we live at the start of the twenty-first century, maybe our lifestyle is more the sham. The junk culture that surrounds us, and the way mediocrity is lauded in all aspects of life, would never have been tolerated fifty years ago. Pop stars and footballers being paid millions for doing just another job of work would have been sneered at. Buying products just because they bear a certain 'designer' label, rather than because of what they actually are, wouldn't have happened. With record numbers of people in debt, millions having to take tranquillisers to cope with just getting through the day, widespread social problems . . . is it us today, or was it those in the past, fooled? With an average now of five television sets per household, all spewing out advertising hype which many people actually believe,

Princess Diana meets crowds outside the Brighton Centre, 1990 – see page 138

generating an increasingly grabbing, must-have-it-now lifestyle, we have surely been infinitely more deceived than they ever were.

Christopher Horlock
October 2000

THE BEACH AND PALACE PIER

This second look at Brighton during the twentieth century starts with this lively, crowded view of the Palace Pier and central beaches. The pier opened as the Brighton Marine Palace and Pier in May 1899, with plans for a light railway to run down the centre, but this never materialised. The theatre opened in April 1901 and staged every kind of show over the years – concerts, plays, pantomimes, operettas, ballet (the great Pavlova appeared once) and even a circus.

On the beach, pleasure yachts – 'Any more for the Skylark?' – are filling up for short trips out to sea and on the promenade, stalls sell every kind of shellfish. Very few people are actually in the water, except those glimpsed by the bathing machines. This is Brighton fulfilling its role of providing simple seaside fun for the thousands of trippers who packed the town each summer.

THE BEACH BRIGHTON

A 112-page guidebook of 1900, puts all the emphasis on the beaches, piers and seafront entertainment plus trips out from the town. Visiting the Pavilion comes way down the list and taking in the town's unique architecture isn't even mentioned! Lewes Crescent at Kemp Town, gets only half a line!

REMAINS OF THE CHAIN PIER

At the turn of the century, remains of Brighton's old Chain Pier, which stood opposite New Steine could still be seen at low tide. The pier had opened in October 1823, as an embarkation jetty for steamers to and from France, in the years of peace following the end of the Napoleonic wars. When blown down in a storm in December 1896, the wreckage caused huge damage along the entire seafront, wrecking the West Pier, Volk's Railway and the Palace Pier, which was being built to replace it. Most of the debris was bundled up and sold off in a series of auctions held on the beach. It is said that some of the old pier's timbers were still in place until the 1930s, but there seems no definite confirmation of this.

The smaller view shows the sundial and other relics of the Chain Pier displayed on the Palace Pier in the early 1900s.

THE WEST PIER

In 1900, the Palace Pier was less than a year old and hardly had a feature on it. The West Pier had opened thirty-four years earlier (1866) and was fully appointed with extensive landing stages, a theatre, bandstand, kiosks and amusements of all kinds. All was well with the pier until the post-war period, when neglect by its owners, the impact of television and the decline of tourism all took their toll and it was fully closed in 1975.

The huge lamp posts date from 1893, when the seafront was lit by electricity. When proposed, one councillor claimed they were tall enough to light Mars! They still stand on the seafront, but with different tops, seen on page 61. The lanterns that hang from the posts today are replicas, installed early in 1983.

SEINE FISHING

If conditions were right, trippers on the beach might see fishermen suddenly spring into action and land a catch in a matter of just a few minutes. This would be seine fishing, where shoals of mackerel swimming close to the shore were quickly surrounded by netting let out from rowing boats, then dragged straight onto the beach, in one quick operation.

The view of this dates from about 1905. The Brighton fishing community was very close-knit and made up of large families who had fished for generations. As can be seen, children learned the trade from a very young age.

In the 1950s, the council considered the fish-market building, housed in arches on the lower promenade, to be out of date and unhygienic. A move to Circus Street early in 1960, to premises alongside the fruit and vegetable market (seen on page 71), was complied with, but deeply resented.

THE LIFEBOAT
In the early 1900s, Brighton had a lifeboat station on the lower promenade, between the piers. This was where the William Wallis, seen here about 1910, was kept. The boat was acquired by the town in December 1904. It is seen going through a demonstration launch, opposite the Grand Hotel, the main event of a 'Lifeboat Saturday', when the boat would be paraded along the seafront (on a carriage, pulled by horses) then launched with full crew, in order to raise funds for the RNLI.

As always, before television (and even radio at this time), thousands of spectators were attracted by such events.

Brighton continued to have a lifeboat on its seafront until August 1932. Now, the town's lifeboat is stationed at the Marina with another lifeboat based at Shoreham.

AEROPLANE RACE

An exciting new experience for visitors at this time was being buzzed by primitive aircraft coming over from Shoreham, where an aerodrome existed from early 1911. The main photograph shows an important early aerial event; a cross country race from Brooklands to Brighton in May 1911.

Only four airmen entered – Gustav Hamel in a Bleriot monoplane, D Graham Gilmour in a Bristol biplane (seen in the main picture), Lt Snowden Smith in a Farman biplane, and CH Pixton in an all-British Roe biplane. The finish was marked by a balloon, fixed near the Palace Pier. Hamel won an £80 prize, but Snowden Smith, who came second,

was disqualified for going the wrong way. Graham Gilmour was therefore awarded second place with a £30 prize, donated by Harry Preston, owner of the Royal York Hotel. All these men were great aviation heroes at this time and feted like footballers and film stars are today. But flying was a risky business; in 1914, while flying from Boulogne to Hendon, Hamel crashed into the Channel and, despite an extensive search (four destroyers, a naval cruiser, a flotilla of gunboats and two seaplanes), neither he or his aircraft were found.

FIRST SPEED TRIALS

More mechanical marvels – this time on the ground. It's July 1905, and Brighton is holding its first 'Motor Race Week'. The start, seen here, was at the very eastern end of Madeira Road (now Drive), near the terminus of Volk's Railway. Number 1 Madeira Terrace, in the background of the main view, was removed in 1932.

Harry Preston was a key promoter of these first speed trials. After huge opposition from Brighton Corporation, the seafront road received a full tarmac surface (the first in the town) and a week's racing was sanctioned on an experimental basis. The 'racing' was essentially to see who could go fastest over a fixed mile.

Those taking part would nearly all become legendary and the list reads like a roster of motoring and sporting greats; CS Rolls (of Rolls-Royce), Sir Ralph St George Gore, T Schneider (seen in the main view, and founder of the Schneider Trophy Races), JTC Brabazon and A Lee Guinness.

The highest speed reached was 90.2 mph, by SF Edge in a 90hp Napier.

The finishing line for the town's first speed trials is seen above, not far from the Aquarium and Palace Pier. The trophies for winners of various categories are also pictured. This early race meeting was certainly not a 'lads only' event. Several women took part and the fastest over the mile was 'plucky Miss Levitt', who came fourth with a top speed of 77.6mph. Some lady!

Madeira Walk and Terrace, in the background of the main view, where the spectators are, was built between 1890 and 1897, following the opening of the lift and shelter hall (far distance) in May 1890.

The noise generated by the early cars caused tremendous hostility from residents and hotel owners along the seafront: 'the roar of engines likening to the sound of an artillery volley,' was a comment in the local press. In fact, opposition to the trials was such that no further meetings took place in Brighton until the early 1920s, and it would be 1932 before a full-scale event was held on Madeira Drive again.

THE AQUARIUM

Today, Brighton's Sea-Life Centre occupies premises that were originally the town's Aquarium, opened in August 1872. The Victorians became obsessed with natural history, due to exotic animals being brought to Britain from far away places by explorers, and of course, Darwin's revolutionary ideas about evolution, set out in *On The Origin Of Species*, published in 1859.

Brighton's Aquarium was the work of Eusebius Birch, who

had also designed the West Pier. It was originally planned to house the aquarium under the pier's entrance. A grander site was later chosen, occupied then by the main entrance to the Chain Pier, seen in the smaller view.

This pier stood at the end of a very long, curving carriageway, below New Steine. This entrance and road were done away with when Madeira Road was laid out from 1870, followed by the building of the Aquarium two years later.

The clock tower was added in 1874.

INTERIOR OF THE AQUARIUM

A view of the main corridor inside the Aquarium, about 1908, showing how the tanks for the exhibits were arranged. One of these was 110 feet long and held up to 110,000 gallons of water, housing (in 1900) porpoises. The Aquarium was extremely popular as it was possible to spend a whole morning or afternoon in the building for sixpence. Lectures, organ recitals, orchestral concerts, variety turns and all manner of novelties were laid on to attract people inside. It was among the most popular attractions on the seafront for some fifty years (along with the piers), declining after World War One.

VARIETY ACTS AT THE AQUARIUM

'Gloriously tacky', might be the best phrase to describe the incredible assortment of novelty acts that appeared on the small, 22 foot stage at the Aquarium, crammed in at the end of a row of tanks.

In late Victorian times we know snake charming, rifle shooting and mechanical ducks could be seen, and Don Pattos 'the marvellous and world-renowned, one-legged Spanish dancer', did his 'celebrated dance'. Louis Lavater turned somersaults while playing the violin, Walter Stanton was 'the human farmyard', and Madame Alphonsene, on a large sphere, rolled up planks arranged over the rockery situated at the far, eastern end of the building.

Weird animal acts, midgets, giants, 'The Tiger Lady', 'The Missing Link', as well as the usual acrobats, magicians, ventriloquists, opera singers, plate spinners, monkey and dog acts, etc, all held the stage at the Aquarium at the turn of the century. Unfortunately, photographs of these 'turns' are rare. One here shows 'Cocky', a talking parrot, who held fast, witty conversations with his owner. The other is Monsieur Beaute, the 'Continental Fasting Man', who was at the Aquarium in March 1906, fasting for three weeks. People paid to see him sitting in a cement hut, living on just cigarettes and mineral water. He lost ten pounds in the first week and continued for just over three weeks. 'He did not look much the worse for it,' wrote one observer. All this was entertainment in Brighton a hundred years ago!

DIAVOLO

Another extraordinary act to appear at the Aquarium, about 1903, was Diavolo, who looped-the-loop on a bicycle. Note the large assortment of nets and mattresses ready to catch him if he came off, plus the padded suit to protect him if he missed any. Preparing his act must have taken hours, yet was all over in seconds.

A later variation was his 'Devil's Wheel', 15ft in diameter, which rotated like a giant hamster wheel. He would try to circle the inside by going upside down, usually getting 90 per cent round (to huge applause of course). Then he would transfer to the outside, balancing on top, pedalling furiously to hold his position and sweating profusely because of all the padding. To finish, he would

suddenly fly off, landing on one of the mattresses, then take his bow. Again, not a particularly long act one feels!

These Aquarium novelty acts seem a world away from the sophisticated entertainment on offer today, but in the early 1980s, there was a sideshow at one of Brighton Marina's early open days, where a woman descended into a tank and wrestled sharks. This was exactly the sort of act the Aquarium would have booked, eighty years earlier.

KING'S ROAD

In 1821 George IV, the town's most famous resident, actually paid for a proper roadway to be laid on a seafront track. The road was named in his honour and he opened it in January 1822. This picture shows the road about 1908, easily recognisable today as many of the buildings remain. A tarmac surface would be laid down in the summer of 1910. The large store on the left is Barrance and Ford, outfitters, at the corner of Middle Street.

RUSSELL STREET

It's hard to believe this view was taken just off Brighton's famous seafront. This is Russell Street, about 1912, which ran up from King's Road, west of West Street, towards Western Road. It was fairly near the Grand Hotel. The map on page 78 gives the exact location. At the top, at right angles, was Upper Russell Street, where the Good Intent pub can be made out.

The bustle is due to the large building on the left being used as a meat store at this time. Originally it was the Church of the Holy Resurrection, built in 1828. The meat store obviously supplied hotels and large shops; the central cart in the foreground has 'Equitable Co-Operative' under the front awning. The main Co-Op store was in London Road, but it was a much smaller building than the huge department store there today.

The turning to Russell Place can be seen by the curved lamp bracket on the right. This street is seen on page 79. Russell Street survived until 1969. The site today is covered by the Brighton Centre and the Churchill Square car park.

WEST STREET

Our survey moves to the old town area now. West Street, part of the main thoroughfare from the station to the sea, is seen about 1905. St Paul's Church is the only recognisable feature. This was built in 1848, with the tower a much later addition of the 1870s. It was a 'Wagner' church, one of eleven built for the town during the Victorian period by the Vicar of Brighton, Henry Wagner and his son, the Reverend Arthur Wagner, who was perpetual curate of St Paul's. The Church of the Resurrection, seen two pages back in Russell Street, was another of these churches.

This is one of those amazing views where people are seen walking anywhere they like because there is simply no traffic to worry about.

WEST STREET BREWERY

Just out of sight, to the left in the previous view, was the entrance to the West Street Brewery, of which this is the only known photograph, dating from about 1910. It had been founded in 1767 by Isaac Grover, who owned the Seven Stars in Ship Street, and whose grandfather had brewed in North Street the previous century. Vallance and Catt, another long-established brewery, took over in September 1895, but brewing ceased in 1913, when the brewery was taken over again, this time by the firm of Smithers.

It was a significant building in the area as it was the first site bought by the corporation, in 1929, for a proposed redevelopment between Western Road and the seafront (bordering onto West Street). This was planned in the 1930s, but didn't actually take shape until the 1960s, in the form of Churchill Square, the car park off Regency Road and the Top Rank building, with the Brighton Centre following in the 1970s.

The brewery went in 1933 and the SS Brighton sports stadium went up on the site straight away. This was demolished in 1966 and today the Quality Hotel has been built on the site of the ancient brewery.

NORTH STREET

Moving to the top of West Street (just beyond the horse bus), we see a real hive of activity, looking across North Street from the corner of Queen's Road Quadrant, about 1908. You can almost hear the clatter and creak of the horse bus as it lurches down North Street and the babble of chatter as people go about their business. This has to be one of the most atmospheric and evocative of all the pictures taken in Brighton before World War One. The background is dominated by the huge store owned by the firm Soper's, founded in 1860.

THE UNICORN INN

This is the imposing Unicorn Inn, near the top of North Street, on the northern side, about 1912. The horse bus on the previous page was just about to pass it. Windsor Street is on the right and the Clock Tower would be just around the corner on the left. The site today is largely occupied by the Boots store, built in 1979.

The Unicorn Inn dates from 1893 and replaced an earlier inn of the same name on the site, part of which was originally a farmhouse dating from 1597. When the conversion was made, early in 1892, the remains of a well were unearthed, believed to be the main town well in Elizabethan times.

The inn here stood for only twenty-seven years. In 1920, together with extensive stabling and properties in Windsor Street and Queen's Road, it was demolished to make way for the Regent Cinema. The main frontage for this was in Queen's Road, but a smaller, side entrance would cover the site of the inn.

EAST STREET – BRILL'S BATHS

The 1860s and 1870s saw many key amenities provided for visitors, following the arrival of the railway from London to Brighton in 1841, and the subsequent popularity and expansion of the town. The Grand Hotel, the West Pier, Brill's Baths (seen here), the Aquarium and several unique churches all date from this period.

Brill's Baths, of 1869, near the southern end of East Street, backing on to Pool Valley, provided a range of

bathing, swimming and leisure facilities (a reading room, billiards, smoking room, hairdressers etc) and played a very significant part in the social life of the well-to-do in late Victorian Brighton.

Designed by Sir George Gilbert Scott (of St Pancras Station fame), and built at a cost of £80,000, it was a bright red brick building, and would have been even bigger and more grand had finances permitted. An interior view is on page 65.

Prominent in the background is the Greyhound Inn, which is now named The Fishbowl. This was called The Anchor in mid-Victorian times and was rebuilt in 1929.

The buildings on the left, in shadow, came down as recently as 1984, when the Queen's Hotel was extended to border on to East Street.

THE TOWN HALL

The middle of East Street is seen here, about 1905, with Brighton's Town Hall, in Bartholemews, dominating the view. This was designed by Thomas Cooper and built between 1830 and 1831. Cooper also designed the original Bedford Hotel, burnt down in April 1964. His Town Hall building survives today, despite many attempts to demolish it in the twentieth century, particularly since the war.

As can be seen, Bartholomews resembled London's Covent Garden in the early part of the century (smaller view). This was due to Brighton's fruit and vegetable market still being located in Market Street at this time.

The market is glimpsed in the distance (the low building, with the curved pediment), built in bright red brick and terracotta, between 1900 and 1901.

REBUILDING OF THE MARKET

Brighton had received a market charter as far back as July 1313, during the reign of Edward II, and there were many market buildings in Market Street over the years, hence its name. This photograph of 1900 shows an old 1830 market coming down on the western side of the street, directly opposite the Town Hall, which is just out of sight by the cart. A new market building is being constructed as the old one is cleared.

This new building is the one glimpsed on the previous page and was designed by Francis May, Brighton's Borough Engineer.

The smaller view shows an initial drawing of the 1900 building, looking from more or less the same viewpoint as the photograph.

The market would open in August 1901, comprising three long, glass-roofed bays, two for fruit and vegetable sales and one for the sale of flowers, seen on the next page.

THE FLORAL HALL

This view is inside the new market's Floral Hall and looks eastwards towards Market Street. Although the hall mostly sold flowers, much in demand by the town's hotels and to dress civic functions and concerts, it also had stalls selling china, stationery items and fancy goods. 'The handsome Floral Hall,' commented a Brighton review of 1911, 'where an abundance of beautiful flowers and plants is always provided, is a great attraction to visitors and townspeople alike. Through the arched glass roof abundant light is admitted, enabling the artistically composed bouquets and foliage groups to be displayed to complete advantage.' One can only wonder what the smell was like, walking through.

MIDDLE STREET SCHOOL

Two streets away from Market Street, westwards, is Middle Street, with its historic school, seen here in 1905. The school originally stood on just the western side of Middle Street, near the turn into Duke Street (just out of sight on the right). The school was founded in 1805, the year of the Battle of Trafalgar, and was first known as the Union Charity School. It was run by a committee from three neighbouring churches – the Countess of Huntington's, North Street, the Salem Baptist Chapel, Bond Street and the Union Street Chapel.

At first it was just for boys, but after operating for three years, girls were admitted. It was a free school until 1821; small fees were then charged to cover expenses. In 1874, it was taken over by the School Board and the building was extended southwards, facing into Boyces Street, with a new façade added (the one seen here) to the Middle Street section. All this was cleared in two phases during 1971, and replaced by the present school building on the site.

NEW ROAD

This view of New Road, from the North Street end, dates from about 1900. The buildings on the left date from 1820, fourteen years after the road was laid out. The women's clothing business of Homer Herring, established in 1879, would later move to 3-4 New Road and continue trading until 1974.

As can be seen, the covered walkway – the Colonnade – used to extend from the Theatre Royal, round to North Street, where it stopped outside number 157, just below King Street. The section beyond the lamp standard was removed in September 1912, the corner section in June 1929.

The horse bus to the right belongs to the firm run by Walter Tilley and is travelling between Castle Square and Lewes Road, a route that had started in August 1872. Again note the absence of all other kinds of traffic.

THE THEATRE ROYAL

The Theatre Royal in New Road, Brighton's most distinguished and lauded theatre, opened in June 1807, simply named the New Theatre. In 2007, the building will be 200 years old. It cost £12,000 to build and originally held more people – some 1,200, compared with 952 today. The present red-brick frontage, with its small octagonal turrets, dates from 1894. The interior was last remodelled in the 1920s.

The main picture shows the theatre about 1908. The scene below is from a popular musical, The Arcadians, which played the theatre in November 1910. It was produced by Robert Courtneidge, father of Cicely, the popular variety performer.

ALIAS JIMMY VALENTINE

A scene from the play *Alias Jimmy Valentine*, which was at the Royal in May 1911. This was about a criminal, whose special talent was opening safes, purely by sense of touch. Early in the play he is arrested and seems destined for a long sentence behind bars, but there is insufficient evidence to convict him.

The scene here is much later in the play, when Jimmy is a reformed character – a bank manager no less! When a child is accidentally trapped in

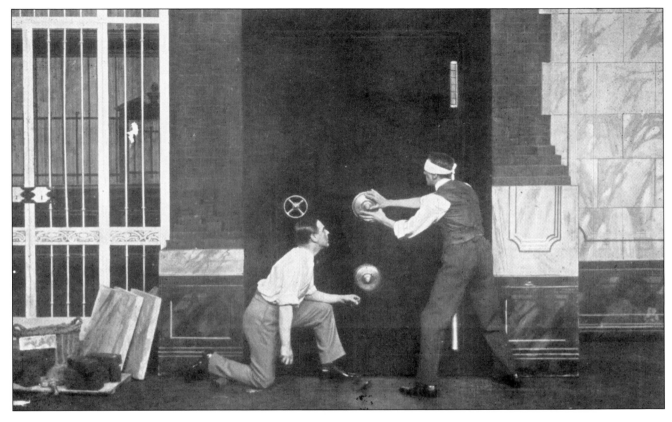

the main safe, he has to resort to his old skills to open it up. Unfortunately, the blindfold he wears (he works by sense of touch, remember) prevents him seeing a detective enter, who watches him at work. The child is freed, but the detective now has the evidence needed to secure the original conviction.

Exciting stuff? The critic of the *Brighton Herald* didn't think so. 'The great criminal detective play,' he wrote, 'will be found to be quite a primitive affair, with more of ingenuousness than ingenuity; you see it comes from America.'

THE LAST HORSE-DRAWN MAIL COACH

Transport in Brighton was revolutionised during the first few years of the twentieth century. Horse-drawn vehicles, particularly buses, were suddenly jostling for road space with trams (from November 1901) and motor buses (December 1903), then all manner of commercial vehicles and eventually, of course, early cars.

The picture here shows the very last mail stagecoach about to leave the Ship Street Post Office,

before being replaced by a motor vehicle. This was in June 1905. The driver is very well wrapped up against the elements – although whatever the weather, the journey northwards over Clayton Hill would have been very arduous.

The Royal Mail had been founded in 1635, during the reign of Charles I. The first Post Office opened in Brighton was at the seafront end of Middle Street, on the eastern side, in 1750.

THE FIRST MOTOR MAIL COACH

This was the replacement vehicle for the old stagecoach on the previous page – a brand new motor van. The ER on the side stands for Edward Rex, Edward VII being king at this time. The driver must certainly have welcomed the proper cab to sit in.

The smaller view, of August 1909, shows the van in collision with a lamp standard, while heading back along London Road into Brighton. Behind the scene of the accident is

Springfield Road.

Amusingly, like a corpse, the damaged section of the van has been covered over! Such an incident would have been big news for people in the area with postcards published showing the scene, as a memento of the event.

BREWERY FIRE

Another dramatic event made into souvenir postcards was this fire at Abbey's Brewery store, at the corner of Sutherland Road (left) and Eastern Road (right), which took place in June 1907. Brighton College can be seen in the background and it was only a north-west wind that stopped the fire spreading to the college buildings. Even so, trees in the ground were scorched, windows cracked and blinds were removed to prevent them bursting into flames. Evershed's candle factory, to the north (left), was also threatened.

The upper portion of the store was completely gutted, with 2,300

quarters of malt destroyed, the damage running into thousands of pounds. It was subsequently rebuilt, in exactly the same form, surviving until 1970.

Abbey's Brewery was founded in 1831 and would be absorbed by the well-known Kemp Town Brewery in 1933. Charringtons took over from 1954 and ceased brewing in Brighton in 1964.

PAWNBROKER'S SHOP IN EDWARD STREET

Eastern Road, on the previous page, is a continuation of Edward Street, where this pawnbrokers shop stood, run by TP Lucas, at the corner of Henry Street. The date is about the time of World War One. Business must have been extremely good – there's a staff of six!

Two rather poorly-dressed women appear on the right, showing all the signs of deprivation the area was renowned for at this time. The premises would close and be demolished when the lower part of Edward Street was widened in the 1930s.

Pawnbrokers were basically money lenders. You would take something of value to the shop, leave it there for a fixed period and receive a loan of

money. To retrieve the item, the money had to be repaid, plus interest, once the fixed period was up. If the item wasn't reclaimed in this way, it would be sold in the shop.

GEORGE STREET

Running between Edward Street (in the distance) and St James's Street, George Street retains many of its original buildings, particularly on the eastern (left) side. The shop next to the cart remained a picture-framers until very recently.

The street dates from the 1790s, when the town expanded to the north and north east due to its royal patronage. Behind the line of shops was a fair amount of housing, much of it concealed, but all with entrances from George Street. St James's Court still exists between numbers 1 and 2.

Little George Street, at the northern end, was rebuilt in 1988, retaining four of its original

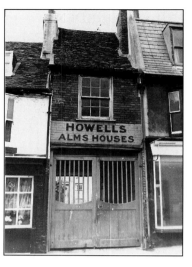

eleven cottages.

Howell's Almshouses were ten tiny, charitable cottages, built in 1858 by Charles Howell. The entrance gate (seen here in 1966) was between numbers 10 and 11. These were all vacated by 1966, but were subsequently demolished, due to their dilapidated state and nothing remains of them today. The gate though, survived until 1987.

DORSET GARDENS

The next street eastwards from George Street is Dorset Gardens, seen here about 1912. This is another very old Brighton Street built, probably, in stages between about 1790 and 1808. It survives in 2000, largely intact, although the southern end (far distance), was redeveloped when Woolworth's, at the St James's Street corner, was extended in the 1960s.

The gardens on the left survive as a small public park, though originally they were private and for the use of the street's residents.

Dorset Gardens church, in among the trees at the far end, dating from 1810, but rebuilt in red brick form in 1884, was demolished in the summer of 2000, and replaced by a community church and a number of flats for the elderly, built by the Guiness Trust.

RICHMOND STREET

Moving further northwards across the town, we see Richmond Street (now Richmond Parade), looking up from Grand Parade. With a gradient of 1:5 it remains the steepest hill in Brighton. The date is about 1912 and the street appears as the jumble of a place people say it was, full of shops, cafes, cobblers, barbers, bakers, butchers, etc., with pubs and beer houses on almost every corner. The wall across the street, seen in the far distance, is said to have been built to stop carts sliding down the hill.

The tower of Richmond Street School can be seen, at the corner of Claremont Row, built in 1873 and demolished as late as 1963, when virtually everything else in the area had been cleared for redevelopment.

The first reference to Richmond Street comes in a directory of 1808. This is probably when early buildings were going up off Grand Parade, work moving progressively eastwards over succeeding years. Census material shows the area then was mostly populated by immigrants.

CHATE'S DAIRY

It's amazing to realise that a farm, originally of thirty acres, existed in the congested Richmond Street area from 1858 until 1934. This was the Richmond Farm Dairy, owned by William Chate, standing on the northern side of the street, on a site today partly occupied by the Chates Farm Court flats. The only surviving building, below, is a wing of the farmhouse at the angle of what remains of Richmond Street and Elmore Road, numbered 34a. Many of the buildings survived as garages until 1977. Chate's grand-daughter, Emily,

recalled that between the wars, some thirty gallons of milk were sold a day in penny and half-penny measures. As well as the cows, there were horses, ducks, chickens, rabbits and homing pigeons, with land ploughed for fodder and growing vegetables.

Chates Farm Court, right, opened in February 1980.

ST JOHN'S WARD CRÈCHE

This picture may not be the early 1900s; it could just be around the time of World War One, but is more likely the 1920s. Either way, it's included in this section as it clearly has to go alongside the previous pictures of Richmond Street, to show further the mixture of occupations taking place in the area. The picture is of a crèche, somewhere in St John's Ward and judging from the incline of the street, it could be Richmond Street itself. The notice on the wall has the times the crèche operated – 7.30am until 8pm, showing the long hours people had to work at this time.

ELM GROVE

Elm Grove, running from Lewes Road to the Race Hill, was given its name in 1852, when the elm trees that line it were planted. This view of about 1905 looks across from Cobden Road, with Elm Grove school, which had opened in 1893, in the background on the left.

Tram lines can be made out in the road. The Lewes Road-Elm Grove route was the first to be constructed when the town's tram system was built, between 1901 and 1904, and was well patronised by crowds

attending meetings at the race course. Thousands could be transported away in a matter of minutes by a line of trams waiting outside the workhouse (now Brighton General Hospital). Many trees still line Elm Grove, particularly at the top, but a fair number went in the 1930s, mostly near the school. This followed an accident when a child, obscured by a tree, ran into the road and was killed by a passing vehicle. Others were lost in the hurricane of October 1987. Those in the foreground here, on the right, have all gone.

The other view is of a tram at the junction of Elm Grove and Queen's Park Road, taken on a wet day in May 1939. The Race Horse Inn, built in 1882, is on the right.

THE RACE HILL

Crowds on the Race Hill, north east of the town, about 1910. Many would have been watching the racing, but often a fair would be held to coincide with race meetings, forming another attraction altogether. All sorts of games of skill, amusements and sideshows would be set up, including displays of freaks, similar to those on show at the Aquarium.

In the background is the wooden Race Hill Mill, at the top of Bear Road, which had been built around 1823 and originally stood off Queen's Park Road, in the area where Windmill Street would be laid out (hence the name). Then, it was named Butcher's Mill, after its owner, Richard Butcher. Financial difficulties saw it sold off and moved to the Race Hill during the winter of 1861-62. It was taken in one piece, minus the sweeps, on a massive iron trailer with five or six huge pairs of wheels, dragged by about twenty horses and thirty oxen. It took the best part of a month to complete the operation, travelling then through largely open countryside, and fortunately, an eye-witness account of the event has survived.

THE RACE HILL WINDMILL

In the early years of the twentieth century, it was still possible to find a number of working windmills in the Brighton area, but being difficult to maintain and with increasing mechanisation taking over milling processes, they were in decline and some, like the Race Hill Mill, were literally on their last legs.

The last owner of the mill was probably George Nicholls, who took over about 1894. Not long after this view was taken the mill was down to two sails (it could still just about operate like this), but it finally collapsed in a cloud of flour dust in May 1913. The central post remained for a year or so, but nothing stands on the site today, which is occupied by a small field used as a horse riding and jumping area. Belle Vue Cottages, in the background, still exist and the site of the windmill is easily traced.

TOWER MILL OFF DITCHLING ROAD

Another windmill to come down in the early 1900s, was the Tower Mill, off Ditchling Road, which originally stood isolated on Round Hill, until surrounded by development from 1870 onwards. The mill was built in 1834 (probably) and was a massive brick structure 60ft high, with four floors and sweeps 32ft long. It cost £2,000 to build and at first had three pairs of grinding stones. In 1829 Charles Cutress bought the mill at auction and a year later, to improve output, had a steam engine fitted and ran a fourth pair of stones. In 1908, the sweeps were removed and the mill ceased working in 1910.

During March and April 1913, the mill was dismantled and many of the bricks were used for building the Belton Road houses that now occupy the site. The day the rubble was finally cleared was the day the Race Hill mill, seen on the previous pages, collapsed.

Cutress would buy the bakers and confectioner's firm owned by a G Forfar of Hove. The firm of Forfars still flourishes in 2000.

DYKE ROAD AND LEWES ROAD

Most roads out of Brighton were undeveloped in the early years of the century. It's hard to believe the top view here is Dyke Road, at the turn of the century. Only the Booth Museum, on the left, opened in 1890, is recognisable. The view looks south down to the Old Shoreham Road. Dyke Road Park would be laid out on land to the right, opening in September 1924.

Barren Lewes Road, below, is seen in 1919. The location is recognisable, despite being open countryside. The railway line to Lewes, crossing the road at this point opened in June 1846. When the Lewes Road became a dual carriageway in 1967 the western arch was 'opened up' and supported by concrete spanning which has spoilt the bridge's proportions to some extent.

THE SEVEN DIALS

Moving back towards the main town area, we see the Seven Dials, about 1905, looking across to Dyke Road and the 150ft tower of the Dials Congregational Chapel, built in 1871 and demolished in 1972.

The name for the area obviously comes from the seven roads that converge at this point, but there seems no definite record of when the name was first used.

The area was mainly built up from the 1840s onwards, quite late compared with other areas of a similar distance from the old town boundaries.

In 1925, there was a serious proposal to install public lavatories in the centre of the roadway at the

Seven Dials. This idea was sensibly dropped, but the first traffic roundabout was put in nine years later.

CABS IN TERMINUS ROAD

Horse cabs line up in Terminus Road, outside the station entrance, in 1903. Ninety-seven years later, the plaques fixed to the wall, just visible, still exist, bearing the letters HCS – horse-cab stand – marking the old waiting places.

The cabs in the picture were unlicensed and had to form a queue up the hill, with only two at a time being permitted on the station forecourt. Licensed cabs were allowed inside the station.

The enormous, curved roof of 1882-1883, seen on the right, would be completely rebuilt and facilities at the station upgraded between 1997 and 2000, at a cost of £28 million.

QUEEN'S ROAD AND STATION

Around the corner from Terminus Road is the main entrance to Brighton Station, seen here around 1908, with a tram outside, ready to take passengers down Queen's Road to Old Steine, via North Road. The smaller view is of a tram interior.

Trams began running in Brighton from November 1901. Various routes were added until the system was completed with the station route in the summer of

1904. Trams provided cheap, efficient public transport in the town, right up to World War Two, when they were withdrawn in favour of trolley buses. A tram interior is shown above.

Property to the left of this view would be cleared in 1924 for the creation of Junction Road. This was sub-sequently widened in 1935.

NORTH ROAD

Another amazingly busy 'people picture', taken by a postcard photographer, somewhere around 1906. This is North Road, about a third of the way up, with Jubilee Street running off to the left. At this time, the surface of North Road was made up of wooden blocks, put down in 1904, when the tram rails were laid. The rails were set on a solid foundation to the level of the road, then wooden blocks were used to fill the spaces around them, mosaic-like, leaving the top of the rails exposed. A thin layer of tar was then spread as a 'top coat', completing the job. Many roads in the town received this treatment when the tram system was being built. When the system was dismantled and the lines removed, people would prise the wooden blocks up and use them as firelighters, particularly those with a coating of tar. North Road was first built up from 1810 and originally was even narrower than it is today. The present road width dates from 1870.

THE PAVILION MILITARY HOSPITAL

Volume I gave details of how many Brighton schools, institutions and large houses were taken over by the military authorities during World War One, to serve as temporary hospitals. This was because existing hospitals would clearly have insufficient room to cope with the number of wounded soldiers sent back from the Western Front via coastal ports along the south. At the suggestion of King George V, the Royal Pavilion, Dome and Corn Exchange buildings were converted into wards for wounded Indian soldiers serv-ing alongside British troops in northern France.

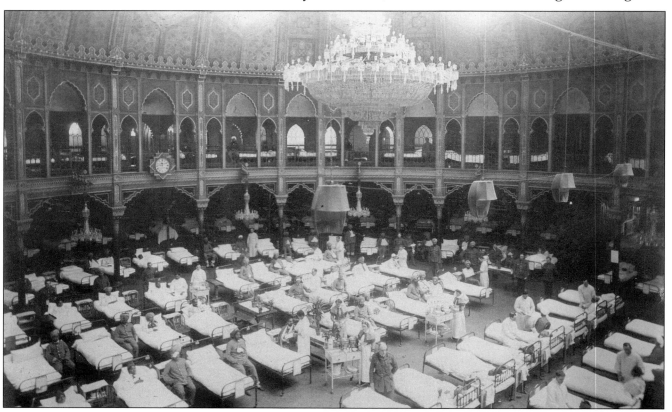

This picture shows the arrangement of beds in the Dome, which originally was an extravagant, circular stable building for the Pavilion Estate, completed in 1808; at this time it was serving as a concert hall (the conversion was made in 1866-67).

Stories of Indians reviving in the Pavilion, and belie-ving they were in heaven because of the sumptuous décor, are quite genuine.

THE KITCHENER INDIAN HOSPITAL

Another building commandeered by the authorities in World War One, was the Brighton Poor Law Institution (previously the Brighton Workhouse), at the top of Elm Grove, at present Brighton General Hospital. This was also initially for wounded Indians, seen about to go for a walk over the Race Hill. They were treated at this hospital for just under a year, arriving in January 1915, but leaving in November the same year, when Indian troops were reassigned to the Mediterranean area. The hospital then took wounded British men, as did the Pavilion Estate.

The problems caused by having the 'men of the Empire' in the town were described in Volume I. Many of those at the Pavilion climbed the temporary wall installed around the grounds to seek out prostitutes in the

Edward Street area. 'I have been very bad here,' one wrote in a letter home. Yet there was huge patriotism and loyalty amongst the Indians ; another letter said: 'If we die on the battlefields for our King, this is equal to entering heaven.'

STANFORD ROAD BOARD SCHOOL

This is one of the schools that became a hospital in Brighton during World War One. Unfortunately, very little detail is known about it. As it has 'Second Eastern General Hospital' over the main entrance, it was presumably an annexe to the Brighton, Hove and Sussex Grammar School hospital, Dyke Road, which also bore the same name but seems to have been the more significant building. It's guessing, but presumably, when the grammar school was full, wounded men were sent here, so the first arrivals were possibly in early September 1914.

Seeing a number of men at the windows could indicate the school was for less severe cases or those not requiring specialist treatment.

AIRCRAFT FACTORY

Two unusual World War One photographs, showing workers at an aeroplane factory at the bottom of Devonshire Place, behind St James's Street.

The top view shows inside the works, and the identity of the moustached man on the left is known. He was James Goldring, who would later become a foreman at the Allen West factory in Lewes Road. The other picture, showing lines of women workers, some holding wing sections, dates from 1917.

Following the war, the factory became a motor coach works.

All kinds of small workshops and factories sprang up rapidly across the country in World War One, making every kind of component to aid the war effort. Women of course, became a key workforce at this time, helping them to secure certain rights – particularly the right to vote – in the years following the war.

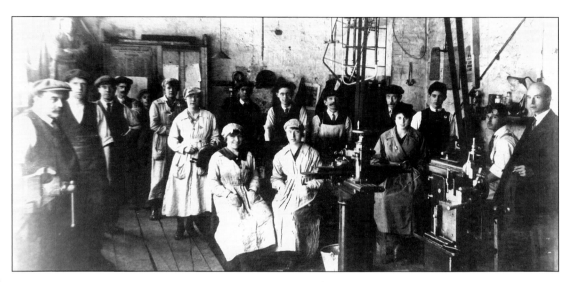

BRIGHTON CARNIVAL

This view could almost show celebrations to mark the end of World War One, but actually moves us into the 1920s period and to the seafront, where the Brighton Carnival procession of June 1923 is taking place. The floats, trade vehicles and performers came along the seafront from the end of Madeira Drive, then up and back along Marine Parade, many spectators viewing the procession from Madeira Terrace.

The first Brighton Carnival had been held in 1922, for a week. Today, the town's carnival still flourishes, organised by the Brighton Lions charity club (who took over the event in 1963), but sets off from the old Hove border, makes its way along the seafront, then winds northwards through the town to Preston Park.

REBUILDING THE AQUARIUM

Brighton Corporation acquired the Aquarium in 1902, but its popularity waned over succeeding years to such an extent that in 1922 an offer by Southdown to turn the site into a coach terminus was approved.

There was huge opposition to this and an application to close the Aquarium was defeated at a public inquiry. Completely capitulating, the Corporation decided to demolish and rebuild a large part of the building, installing new amenities to make the place more profitable.

The picture here, of November 1928, shows the entrance coming down, which was the last part of the demolition to be completed. Beyond, the new building was virtually finished. Removing the clock tower was done simply by

tying ropes to it and pulling hard. Many think that the clock was subsequently installed in a new tower above the entrance to the Palace Pier in 1930, but careful examination of photographs reveals it's not the clock from the Aquarium.

OPENING OF NEW AQUARIUM

'An ornament of which the town may be justly proud,' was how one local paper greeted the rebuilt Aquarium, seen here the day it was opened by Prince George (inset), later Duke of Kent, in June 1929.

Inside, forty of the original tanks had been retained, but the huge 110ft tank had been converted into thirteen smaller ones. The building now housed a multi-purpose concert hall (the Prince's Hall), equipped with a projection box so that films could be shown. It could be converted into a dance hall if needed, larger than the Regent in Queen's Road. There was a range of bathing facilities, plus a 30ft rifle range, serving as headquarters for the Imperial Rifle Club. The roof had three terraces on different levels, linking up with Marine Parade, Madeira Terrace and Madeira Drive.

RUSSELL STREET

Russell Street, seen earlier on page 21, is glimpsed now in the mid-1920s, looking up from King's Road. This viewpoint reveals the entrance to the Palladium, on the right, which operated from 1888 as a music hall, the Alhambra, then from 1912 until 1956 as a cinema. The seafront entrance (a converted shop), was seen in Volume I. Further up, left, the Cannon Brewery with its chimney can be made out. Nothing here now exists, the street was cleared intermittently following World War Two, final clearance coming in 1969. The site is covered by the Brighton Centre and the Churchill Square car park.

Russell Street dated from the late 1780s and took its name from Dr Richard Russell, the Lewes physician, who advocated bathing in the sea to relieve glandular disorders. This brought many wealthy visitors to Brighton from the 1750s, including King George IV, beginning its popularity as a seaside resort.

OLD SHIP, EXETER AND HOLLYWOOD HOTELS

This 1920s view is where Black Lion Street emerges at King's Road. It shows three seafront hotels, one next to the other; the eastern end of the Old Ship is on the left, the Exeter Hotel is in the centre, and the Hollywood Hotel stands on the extreme right, bordering on to Market Street, which was the next street eastwards. The site of these was where, over succeeding years, any number of plans would come and go for a new town hall, to replace the old, outmoded 1830s one in Bartholomews. Models and drawings of some of these proposals are included later in the book. None of them would come to anything, for one reason or another, until the building of the Ramada Renaissance Hotel in the 1980s, which incorporated a civic centre on three sides behind it, housing new council offices.

KING'S ROAD AND WEST STREET

An unusual view of King's Road, at the turn into West Street, probably dating from 1929. The seafront lamps are now two hanging lanterns, installed in the spring of 1928, when the boundaries of the town dramatically changed and Greater Brighton was created. This event is fully described in Volume I.

At the bottom of the picture, a post can be made out, which is the top of the first traffic-signalling device installed in

Brighton, during December 1927. In involved levered arms being raised electronically by a policemen installed in a nearby rotunda-type control box (the small view). Previously policeman would have stood in the road and given hand signals. Other signalling units were subsequently installed at Preston Circus, the Seven Dials and Old Steine. The first traffic lights in Brighton came into operation during 1933.

The line of buildings seen here would come down early in 1963, and be replaced by the Top Rank entertainment centre, presently the Kingswest building.

WEST STREET

West Street in the 1920s was lively, but rundown, smelling of the sausage and mash shops that lined it, a real tripper route to and from the station. It was also extremely narrow and widening for the increasing demands of 20th century traffic was long overdue. This would begin in 1925 at the top, western corner, the whole line of property on the western side (left in this view) coming down over succeeding years and relined with modern buildings in a more uniform style. The exception was St Paul's Church, which was already set back. The vicarage for the church was then the building on the extreme left. This came down in 1933, but the whole widening and rebuilding did not reach the seafront end until the 1960s.

NORTH STREET

This is the eastern end of North Street in the 1920s, seen from opposite the end of New Road. Hannington's store can be seen on the right side of the road in the distance (beyond the lamp), but the street is dominated by the huge electrical store on the left, which formed a serious bottleneck for traffic between Princes Place and Castle Square. This store and adjoining property would come down in 1930 for the building of Prince's House, occupied today by a restaurant.

On the right a man has just passed one of several Lyons restaurants in the area. Most of these shut in the mid-1970s, when the closure of Lyons bakery at Hove was imminent, with production due to be centralised at new premises at Carlton, near Barnsley.

EAST STREET

This is the southern part of East Street in 1925, looking from the corner of Bartholomews, down towards the sea. The curved building still exists, operating as a shoe shop.

This part of East Street has remained narrow and small in scale, retaining much old town character and atmosphere.

At the corner of Pool Lane, on the eastern side, stood the massive Brill's Baths, the north west corner of which is seen in the smaller view.

INTERIOR OF BRILL'S BATHS

A rare photograph taken inside Brill's Baths, about 1925. Judging from the goal on the left, a water polo match has just taken place. This was the main pool in the building, 60ft across, holding 80,000 gallons of water. The surrounding balcony could take up to 400 spectators.

Although the baths had been an immensely successful all-weather amenity for the town in their day, the huge size of the building had become an economic handicap by the 1920s. Medicinal baths were becoming outmoded and new,

up-to-date bathing facilities had just opened in the new Aquarium. The building was operating really just as a swimming pool and café, and the decision was made to close it down and use the site for a new, deco-style cinema. Demolition came early in 1929, the small view showing the domed roof above the main pool about to be broken up.

SIR HERBERT CARDEN AND 'THE CITY BEAUTIFUL'

The redevelopment of the Aquarium and the Brill's Baths sites were radical changes to two key amenities in Brighton. There were many others during the 1920s and 1930s and this period was one of almost non-stop change and improvement for the town. Substantial road widening took place, huge areas of slum property were cleared, trams were replaced by trolley  buses, the London to Brighton railway line was electrified, more new cinemas went up, an ice rink opened in West Street, new parks and schools appeared, vast housing estates were developed off the Lewes Road and at Whitehawk ; the list seems endless.

One person who whole-heartedly agreed with sweeping away the old and outmoded buildings of the town was Herbert Carden. He was a radical and charismatic councillor, who helped pull Brighton into the twentieth century after years of lethargy and stagnation. As detailed in Volume I, he spent thousands of pounds of his own money, securing land around the periphery of Brighton, so it was kept from outside development and used to serve the expanding town's precise needs. When projects were decided on, he sold the land to the Corporation, at exactly the price he paid for it, which obviously kept their costs exceptionally low.

Carden was not just interested in the outskirts of Brighton; he had an extraordinary plan, of mind-boggling proportions, for how the seafront area should be developed. He envisaged Brighton as a city, with a whole new frontage, in art deco style, stretching from Shoreham to Newhaven. The view over shows how it all was to look. In May 1935 he wrote: 'The seafront will become the great promenade of the city. The barren stretches of beach which mar the view seawards must be turned into sunken gardens with bathing pools. The cheap stalls must disappear with all that makes for ugliness. Stately new buildings must arise – noble buildings, fine hotels, modern flats and imposing houses. What a chance lies here if we have the courage to grasp it! What a city of Brighton we can build! A city worthy of the finest site in the empire. Shall we plan along these lines and hand over to posterity the city beautiful, or shall we still think of day trippers and whelk stalls as the destiny of Brighton? Is it too much to hope that the next twenty-five years will see this city of Brighton an ideal worthily obtained?'

Several buildings, such as Embassy Court, Black Rock bathing pool and Marine Gate were built along the lines Carden favoured, but his grandiose ideas died with him in 1941. It's fascinating to speculate what might have been if he had lived longer.

TOWN HALL PROPOSAL

One preoccupation of Carden, wholeheartedly shared by most of his fellow councillors, was that Brighton should have a new town hall and civic centre, to replace the old and overcrowded building in Bartholomews, seen on page 27.

This model of 1935 shows a proposal favoured by Carden, which would have stood on the seafront, between Black Lion Street (left) and Market Street (right), exactly where the hotels on page 60 stood. The frontage would have been 300ft in length and set back 60ft from the existing building line. The cost was estimated at £30,000. It was never built, mainly due to wrangling over the site, which was hotly debated at the time. Even the *Brighton and Hove Herald* weighed in with a suggestion for an alternative site, near the Royal Pavilion, seen in the diagram, but nothing came of this either and World War Two put an end to the matter for a number of years.

THE SAVOY CINEMA

The Savoy, which replaced Brill's Baths, was the second 'super-cinema' to be built in Brighton (the Regent in Queen's Road was first) and was designed by William R Glen, FRIAS. It had seating for nearly 3000 people, two restaurants, two cafés and a large garage in the basement for 300 cars.

It opened in August 1930, with a programme of all-British films, including the feature Loose Ends, and the musical burlesque, *Not So Quiet On The Western Front*. *Pathé Super News Gazette* and *Pathé Tone Weekly* were also shown and Quentin Maclean entertained at the Savoy Wonder Organ.

The photograph shows the entrance at the junction of East Street and Pool Lane (left), exactly where the photograph of Brill's Baths on page 64 was taken.

The cinema changed names several times over succeeding years, becoming the ABC in 1963 and the Cannon in 1986. Cannon Cinemas invested in an eight-screen complex at Brighton Marina, which opened in May 1991, leaving the future of the East Street cinema in doubt. Plans to convert it into an £8 million casino were finalised in October 1999, closure finally coming in January 2000.

DEMOLITION OF FLORAL HALL AND MARKET

In the rush to modernise Brighton in the 1920s and 1930s, the market building on the western side of Market Street was considered out of place and causing too much traffic congestion. Accordingly, the Corporation decided it should close and a new one open on a site more accessible to delivery vehicles. The photographs here, probably dating from 1939, show the exterior of the Floral Hall and market about to be cleared (main view), plus the interior of the hall gutted. Much of the site was subsequently used as a car park, staying that way until the late 1980s, when the southern section of Market Street through to Black Lion Street was redeveloped for building the Ramada Hotel and new civic centre.

OPENING OF NEW MARKET

A new market building, replacing the one seen on the previous page, was opened in Circus Street by Deputy Mayor, Edward Denne, in January 1937. The plaque he unveiled can still be found in one of the market bays near the northern end. The cost of the building was £75,000.

The Sussex Street Schools can be seen above the roof line, with the Milner flats

on the right.

Today, the market still operates, but is a very run-down building threatened with closure.

REBUILDING THE DOME INTERIOR

Herbert Carden, in his zeal for improving the town and rebuilding much of it in deco style, even went so far as suggesting the Royal Pavilion should be demolished, being 'an anachronism of our modern age'. Nothing happened of course, but the interiors of the Dome and Corn Exchange were refurbished during 1934-35.

The old Dome concert hall held 1,700 people; modernised (seen taking place in the main view) it would take 3,000. The new interior was formally opened in September 1935, by the Mayor, Alderman Sidney G Gibson. Two concerts were given by the London Philharmonic Orchestra, conducted by Sir Thomas Beecham.

Although the floor of the building was raked to allow good views of the new stage, a temporary floor could be installed, on light steel supports, for dancing (as here), exhibitions and bazaars.

The Dome would be completely renovated and modernised again in 1999-2001.

BATHING BELLES

Here, on the Palace Pier, in August 1936, finalists in a bathing belle contest line up for judging. This was the main event of the annual Palace Pier Carnival, which attracted 18,332 people on to the pier.

In May 1986, fifty years after the event, *The Argus* tracked down the winner, a Mrs Sheila Nunneley, living in Southwick, aged 67. She is second from the left in the picture.

Her sister Mona also took part, seen on the right of the line. They were offered parts in the pantomime on the pier that year, leading to work at the London Palladium with the Crazy Gang. Marriage and parenthood brought an end to Sheila's show business career.

SILVER JUBILEE CELEBRATIONS

On May 6, 1935, the country celebrated the Silver Jubilee of George V and Queen Mary, following a reign of twenty-five years.

In Brighton, the firework portraits seen above formed the finale of a display held on the central beaches that evening. Earlier, there had been a mass thanksgiving service in Preston Park, a pageant of transport through the ages on the seafront and a Jubilee Ball at the Royal Pavilion.

From late April, the main streets were lavishly decorated, as here in North Street, looking east. The Countess of Huntingdon's Church can be seen on the right. The first chapel here opened in 1774; this 1871 version came down in 1972 after the spire started to tilt.

NEW FLATS OFF CARLTON HILL

Some building took place on the cleared Carlton Hill and Sussex Street slum sites before World War Two.

The Milner and Kingswood flats went up in the mid-1930s and still stand today. These housed many residents displaced by the slum clearance work that was taking

place in the surrounding area. The Milner flats were first to be built in 1934 (seen here). They were named after Alderman Hugh Milner Black, who was a great advocate of corporation housing. The adjacent Kingswood flats, which take their name from Sir Kingsley Wood, Minister of Health, went up four years later.

The other view is of Sun Street, running between Edward Street (top of picture) and Carlton Hill, which was typical of the many slum streets cleared in the 1930s.

Other 1930s developments in the area were the Circus Street market, described earlier, several clinics in Sussex Street and the five-and-a-half acre Tarner estate.

BUILDING OF NORTH MOULSECOOMB HOUSING ESTATE

The continuous and widespread provision of council housing throughout Brighton, during the 20th century, is a remarkable and probably unrivalled achievement.

In 1900, there was no corporation housing (as it was then called) in Brighton – except for tied workers' houses. A few rows of council houses appeared from 1902 onwards, such as in May and Natal Roads, but the first large estate was at South Moulsecoomb, then outside the borough boundary, started in 1919, when the land was acquired. This was followed by the

Queen's Park estate in 1922, between Elm Grove and Freshfield Road. The huge clearance of slum property in the Carlton Hill, Sussex Street and Richmond Street area led to two more estates being planned to house displaced families, one at North Moulsecoomb, pictured here, another at Whitehawk.

In February 1925, the corporation bought a thirty-six-acre site off Lewes Road, owned by the Earl of Chichester, for the North Moulsecoomb estate. This cost £5,000 and was known locally as 'Beer Shop Field'. The name came from the time when the Lewes railway line was built across the land, in the 1840s, and labourers were sold beer there, to stop them wandering off the worksite for a drink.

The initial work took place from 1926 to 1929. This picture, of about 1932, shows the main streets in place (the houses with dark roofs) and work in progress on newer property to the east.

BUILDING OF WHITEHAWK ESTATE

Housing in the Whitehawk area had begun in the 1880s with the small terrace of cottage-like houses on the southwest side of Whitehawk Road. These still exist and originally had mouldings of open Bibles over the doorways inscribed with lines of text. These were added to in the 1920s along with houses in Hervey and Whitehawk Roads, plus Whitehawk Crescent.

However, it wasn't until 1928 that the nucleus of the Whitehawk estate appeared, with the first sixty houses being

built. Eighty-four more followed the following year.

The main picture shows houses in Whitehawk Avenue under construction; these no longer exist as they were cleared when the estate was rebuilt in the 1970s (page 132).

The church for the estate, St Cuthman's, is seen in Lintott Avenue in 1937, but this received a direct hit from a bomb seven years later, during World War Two, and wasn't rebuilt until 1951-52.

RUSSELL STREET AREA

This Ordnance Survey map of 1930 shows an area of western Brighton, most of which no longer exists. It was redeveloped over a long period, from the 1920s through to the 1970s, for the widening of West Street, the building of the Top Rank entertainment building (later Kingswest), the whole Churchill Square development, various car parks and finally the building of the Brighton centre.

This all involved massive demolition, clearance and rebuilding, with eighteen streets, courtyards and rows of cottages removed, many too small to be named on the map.

All sorts of interesting features can be located. In Russell Street, the meat market, seen on page 21, can be found, as can the brewery and 'picture theatre' seen on page 59.

The very top road, which has no name printed on, is Western Road.

BLUCHER PLACE AND RUSSELL PLACE

Slum streets didn't just exist in the area between Edward Street and Albion Hill. Although this was the largest and most significant congestion of old properties, there were many other isolated streets and rows of old cottages in other places that were condemned as unfit for human habitation during the inter-war years.

Here, the picture below shows Blucher Place, boarded up, ready for clearance. It can be found on the previous page, near the top of the map, below Grenville Place. Most

of these houses, dating from about 1818, went in 1938; for some reason a few were spared and survived until the 1950s.

The other street is Russell Place, which can also be found on the map, behind St Paul's Church. This view looks eastwards. The cottages date from about 1826 and were demolished in 1936 as slum property.

KING'S ROAD PRIOR TO CLOSURE

This rare view of the seafront takes our look at Brighton during the twentieth century into the period of World War Two. It dates from late 1940 or early 1941, and shows King's Road with wartime defences in place (left), just before the seafront area became a defence zone and was closed off to visitors in March 1941. The bus service, seen operating here, would be withdrawn in October 1942

To the right, the frontage of an Odeon cinema can be seen, dating from 1936. This began life as the 1888 Alhambra theatre (seen on pages 25 and 26 of Volume I), which became a cinema in 1912. It survived until 1956 and the site was eventually cleared early in 1963. The eastern wing of the Brighton Centre, opened in 1977, currently occupies the site.

BOMBING OF RAILWAY VIADUCT

These pictures show the results of an amazing bombing incident that took place in May 1943. Twenty-five Focke-Wulf 190s descended onto the town from the south east and dropped more than twenty bombs across a wide area. Twenty-four people died, fifty-eight were seriously injured and 150 houses rendered uninhabitable in a matter of minutes. As the planes swept down, eye-witnesses reported seeing a man on a roof, or at a high window, discharging a revolver at the planes, trying to bring one of them down.

The bomb that hit the railway viaduct spanning the London Road - the last to be dropped – performed an incredible sequence of acrobatics before detonating. It first hit a building in Campbell Road, then was deflected through a garden wall, bounced a couple of times in the road then passed through the front wall of 2 Argyle Villas. It travelled through two rooms in this house and out through a back window, still without going off. The bomb travelled a further sixty feet to a workshop, passed through its first floor, then travelled on to the railway viaduct striking one pillar, then another, before finally going off. The explosion

dislodged the top portion of two arches, bringing down a huge number of bricks and debris, but leaving the railway lines intact, still spanning the gap. The gap was treated very rapidly and within days trains were using the viaduct again.

WARTIME PEOPLE

Three unusual photographs of Brighton people taken during World War Two, which reflect something of the defiant attitude prevalent in the country at this time.

The main picture, of October 1940, shows Betty Ceaplen in her Cromwell Street air raid shelter, having just given birth to an 8lb girl. A poll to name the child showed Faith was the most popular choice. Nurse Amy Ryman turned up to attend the birth on a motorcycle. In 2000, *The Argus* traced Faith, aged sixty and a mother of three, living in Balsdean Road, Woodingdean. Her mother had died in 1977 aged sixty-five. Nurse Ryman died two years earlier, at ninety-five.

Brighton's own 'cheeky chappie', Max Miller, is seen on his bike, with cigarette, tin hat and irrepressible grin. He was the top stand-up comedian in the country at this time and often topped the bill at the Hippodrome during the war.

Harriet, the flower lady, is probably outside Hanningtons, East Street. 'I ain't going to move from

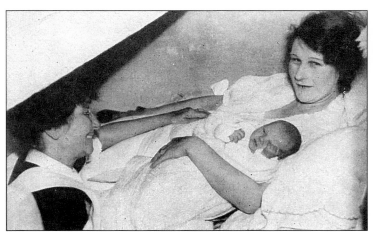

my corner for Hitler or anybody else,' she said to a reporter at this time. 'You just got to die once my duck. I'll be sitting here a long time after Hitler and his bunch are finished.'

She probably was !

WARTIME SAVINGS SCHEMES

During each successive year of World War Two, there were national savings events to buy ships and planes to aid the war effort.

Early in 1940, there was Spitfire Fund Week, with War Weapons Week, following in 1941. Warship Week, the subject of the smaller photograph here, was in October 1942, followed by Wings For Victory Week, in 1943. Salute The Soldier, took place in 1944.

Warship Week saw £760,000 raised and a destroyer, HMS *Kipling*, funded. Unfortunately this was sunk by enemy action in the Mediterranean, but a further appeal raised £730,000 for a replacement.

The main picture shows a large vehicle fitted out as a mobile cinema, which toured the town, promoting these campaigns. It seems to be standing somewhere in the Hanover or Elm Grove area. A short film would have been shown, the flaps on the top and sides of the van would have made the screen area dark, so the picture would have been visible, even on a sunny day. The appeal would probably involve a British film star, asking for contributions; identical films would have been shown in all the local cinemas, too.

STREET PARTIES

Pictures of two of the hundreds of street parties that took place across Brighton to celebrate VE day – Victory in Europe – in May 1945. The large picture was taken in St Paul's Street, off Lewes Road, the other view in Springfield Road, outside Hartley and Midgley's car showrooms. Some of the children here would have witnessed the bombing of the railway viaduct, described a few pages back. A further round of parties took place following the defeat of Japan, in August 1945, bringing World War Two to a final end.

REPAIRING THE WEST PIER

The immediate post-war period in Brighton was a turning point for both the town's history and its future development. The late 1940s saw a substantial falling off in holiday and tripper trade, with the town attracting only 60 per cent of the number it had during the late 1930s. This figure surprises all the more when it's remembered that the first paid weekly holidays for workers in Britain were introduced in 1939, which should have lifted the numbers coming to Brighton after the war, but clearly didn't. The reasons are complex, but essentially to do with the huge disorientation people felt following the war years. A massive slump meant rationing continued, even more austerely than in the war, and there was an acute housing shortage for returning servicemen due to basic materials being unavailable. If people had money, they held on to it. With the detonating of the atomic bomb on Japan and the horrors of the German concentration camps revealed, the world was suddenly a different place in the 1940s. Taking a holiday probably seemed, for many, an almost disrespectful thing to do.

The photograph here, of September 1945, shows the West Pier in two sections; it was cut to prevent any German invasion force using it to take the town. It would re-open in April 1946.

AERIAL VIEW OF SEAFRONT

We move on a few more years, into the 1950s, and see Brighton's seafront and beaches from the air. The enclosures and boating lake near the bottom of the view, west of the pier, were opened in 1925; the paddling pool and putting green, on the other side, in 1938.

The Hotel Metropole, of 1890, stands as originally built, with rooftop pavilions and central spire, removed in 1960 when a restaurant, extra bedrooms and flats were added to the top of the building.

The crowds in the picture seem to indicate all's well for holiday trade at Brighton, but other factors would now take their toll on Brighton's fortunes as a holiday resort.

Britain would now see the rise of car-ownership, camping holidays and holiday camps, which would broaden the choice of holiday people could take, again shifting trade away from seaside resorts. Package holidays abroad would prove increasingly popular. TV ownership rose markedly during the 1950s and people's view of the world was changing, and with it their tastes in leisure and recreation.

CORONATION DECORATIONS

Whatever people's changing ideas on holidays, interest in royal events never abated. Here's Western Road, festooned with decorations to celebrate the coronation of Queen Elizabeth II in June 1953. The view looks eastwards, towards the Clock Tower end. Television was in its infancy in the early 1950s, but some 20 million people watched the coronation on early sets, many specially bought for the occasion.

Below, the *Brighton and Hove Herald* of February 1952 details the proclamation ceremony at the Town Hall.

STREET MUSICIANS

Here, in the summer of 1953, Brighton's two most famous street musicians entertain shoppers in East Street; they were harpist Frederick Alexander and violinist Joseph Marcantonio.

Frederick had come to Brighton from Potenza, Italy, aged eight and teamed up with Joseph in 1900. Joseph had been born in England, of Italian extraction, and in the years before World War One, they played to trippers taking paddle-steamer rides from the piers. After the war they established themselves on Brighton's streets, particularly East Street, Ship Street and Middle Street, where they would entertain the queue of people waiting to get into the Hippodrome. Their fame even took them on to radio and television. Joseph died in 1958, aged seventy-seven. Alexander carried on alone. He died in 1963, aged eighty-four. 'Now the harp's plaintive melodies are stilled and another character of Old Brighton has departed,' wrote *The Argus* at the time.

DAWKIN'S FORGE

Another of Brighton's characters is seen in this view, taken in Marshall's Row, the short street leading to the Open Market from London Road. This is blacksmith William Dawkin, photographed outside his premises in the late 1950s, where shoppers could watch him shoeing horses brought in by tradesmen still using horse-drawn carts. The frame for keeping the horses steady is on the left. The forge had previously been run by Dawkin's father.

William Dawkin died in 1967 and no-one took over the business from him as the need for a smithy was negligible by this time. The forge was auctioned off in 1968 and shops were subsequently built on the site.

GILBERT HARDING

Here in October 1957, at St. John's Church annual sale of work, held in the Riley Hall, Carlton Hill, the author of this book (then four years old) presents a rose buttonhole to Gilbert Harding, who opened the sale.

Harding was the most famous resident of Brighton in the 1950s. Born in a Midland's workhouse where his father presided, he went to Cambridge University, but subsequently took ordinary jobs as a teacher and policeman. He emigrated to Canada, but returned to Britain to help with broadcasting work at the BBC during the war.

The radio show, Twenty Questions, saw his rise to fame, increasing with the famous early TV show, What's My Line? People tuned in just to see Harding and the mood he was in. He could be utterly charming or downright rude by turns, and occasionally appeared drunk. At the Theatre Royal in Brighton, he would often call things out in the middle of a performance, if he didn't think the play or actors were up to it, and people would go to the Royal hoping to hear him heckle.

Harding always stood up for ordinary people though, supported charities and startled everyone when he broke down and cried during a famous TV interview with John Freeman on the programme, Face To Face. Drinking, smoking and ill-health took their toll and he died, aged only fifty-two, on the steps of Broadcasting House, London.

TOWN HALL PROPOSAL
Another plan for a town hall and civic centre on the seafront, between Black Lion Street and Little East Street, virtually the same site of the Carden proposal, seen in the 1930s section.

The date this time is March 1952 and again, as with Carden's idea, the site, bounded by Pavilion Parade and Edward Street, was put forward by some as a better choice and backed by Brighton's Planning Committee. The cost of either site was estimated at £525,000.

Other sites considered were Marlborough Place, York Place, Park Crescent and Withdean Park.

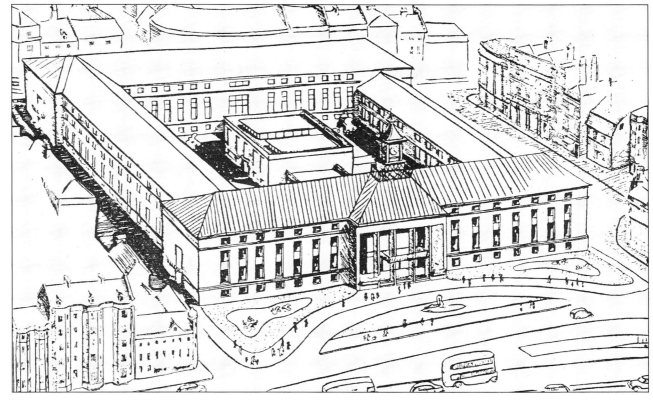

Nothing became of any of them, and again the idea was put into abeyance.

Interestingly, a little earlier, a Five Towns plan was drawn up by the council, in which it was proposed that Brighton, Hove, Portslade, Southwick and Shoreham, plus Peacehaven, should become a Central Sussex Authority. This would have a new civic centre, similar to the one seen here, in either Old Shoreham Road, on the site of Hove Town Hall, at Buckingham Park in Shoreham, or somewhere in Peacehaven.

Needless to say this amazingly radical idea was completely rejected as impractical, unnecessary and not in each town's best interests. It can't be said that councils in the past had no vision!

NORTH ROAD SWIMMING BATHS

This was the town's municipal bathing pool for most of the century, built in 1895. It stood about half way between North Road and Church Street, at the end of Barrack Yard. The main view here dates from June 1957 and possibly shows the annual swimming sports held by the Secondary Technical School in Hanover Terrace, which used the pool for swimming lessons and for inter-house galas. The pool was 120ft by 33ft, contained fresh water, the depth varying from 3ft to 7ft, with more than sixty changing rooms arranged on either side.

The Secondary Technical School began in 1873 as the Hanover Board School. It became the Technical School after World War Two and during the late 1970s served as an annexe of Patcham Fawcett School. Final closure as a school came in July 1981 and, following a brief period as a centre for the disabled, the 127-year-old building was demolished in the spring of 2000 and replaced by housing.

THE GRAND THEATRE

This theatre also stood in North Road, but at the top, near the junction with Queen's Road. It opened in October 1891 as the Hippodrome Circus, with room for more than 5,000 spectators, making it the biggest theatre in Brighton. Two strange acts seen on opening night were Mephisto, a contortionist, known as 'the boneless wonder', and Professor Fredericks miniature circus of performing cats, rats, mice and monkeys. One monkey climbed a rope to the ceiling then floated down on a tiny parachute.

In 1894 the circus became a conventional theatre, the Eden, and was the place to see sensational melodramas. Plays involving murder, suicide, robberies, duelling, shipwrecks, earthquakes, trains colliding, explosions and general mayhem 'packed them in', as did the annual pantomime, with its spectacular scenery and effects.

The theatre became the Grand in 1904, but the full-bloodied fare remained the same. Variety and even nude shows were mixed into the heady brew served up at the Grand, but audiences dwindled when cinemas began to open up. The Grand became a cinema from January 1931, with a brief return to live variety during World War Two. It closed in February 1955 and was a furniture store for a number of years, before burning down in a suitably spectacular fire of June 1961.

CANNON STREET AND ARTILLERY STREET

Two streets that no longer exist; Cannon Street (main view) and Artillery Street, both seen on the 1930s map on page 78 but long since gone for the redevelopment that would become the Churchill Square shopping complex and adjoining car park.

In both pictures the view looks south, towards the seafront. The rear of the Grand Hotel can be made out in both pictures, which helps orientate the viewpoint. Some demolition has already taken place in Cannon Street but full clearance would come for both streets in 1957, following compulsory purchase orders, many of the displaced residents moving to the newly-built Bristol estate at Kemp Town, another of the town's large post-war council estates.

THE HOLLINGBURY ESTATE

From old houses about to come down on the previous page, to new ones going up. This is the Hollingbury estate, photographed about 1950, looking south from Midhurst Rise, down to Carden Avenue (the school can be glimpsed on the left) with County Oak Avenue, on the left, not quite finished.

The Hollingbury estate was the largest post-war housing development in Brighton, built between 1946 and 1951. The first group of 148 houses was built by a co-operative of eighteen local building firms and was reported as 'rapidly moving towards completion', by the local press in October 1946. By 1948, the number of properties had reached 563 and the Carden County Primary Schools had been completed. January 1949 saw the number of houses rise to 658 and the Methodist Church in Lyminister Avenue opened in September 1952. By now, Brighton Corporation was the biggest landlord in Sussex, owning some 8,100 properties overall.

CLEARANCE OF SLUM PROPERTY

During the 1950s the huge back-street area between Edward Street and Richmond Street was a total shambles. As previously described, this had been a slum site, with clearance starting from 1928 and some new buildings going up in the Circus and Sussex Street area in the 1930s. The war and subsequent slump interrupted the redevelopment, so that by the early 1950s, some streets stood totally cleared, some were partly demolished and others, such as Claremont Row (main picture), had old

buildings gone, some still remaining, and prefab housing crammed in the spaces between.

Shells of old houses could be found and sites of others were marked by piles of rubble waiting to be cleared. In Carlton Street (smaller view), one side had been demolished (left), but the other side was intact and still partly occupied, continuing as such until the early 1960s. In this view, the houses in the background still exist, standing in Queen's Park Road, with the Zylo works at the top of Marine View just off to the left.

It wasn't until the early 1960s that large-scale redevelopment took place; flats built, both high and low-rise, characterise the area today.

SUSSEX STREET SCHOOLS

A close-up of the northern end of the Sussex Street Schools, at the end of Claremont Row, one of the last large buildings in the whole slum area to come down. Originally the building was Richmond Street School, dating from 1873, but later amalgamated

with Sussex Street School, which was at the other end of the street, seen on page 71. The whole of the western side of Claremont Row was occupied by these school buildings, with playgrounds in between. Classes were often very large. An inspector's report of 1930 showed that two classes had more than fifty pupils.

The part of the premises seen here was last used as an infants school, but would close in 1962. It was demolished the following year when huge blocks of flats were rising up all around it, such as the one pictured here, to be known as Highleigh, photographed in November 1960.

RICHMOND STREET AREA

September 1966; the area between Edward Street and Carlton Hill has been changed out of all recognition. Six high-rise blocks now dominate the area (described as 'infinitely uncivilised' by the Brighton historian Antony Dale), with four-storey housing built in the Albion Street area. The triangle of land in the distance, to the left, was the site of Chate's Dairy, seen on page 41.

The Tarner estate can also be seen and there's a lot of interest in the foreground of the picture at the bottom of Trafalgar Street. It's clearly playtime at the Margaret Hardy School for girls, part of which was formerly the York Place Elementary Schools, off York Place.

A good photograph of this whole area, prior to redevelopment, can be found in Volume I, page 63.

THE PARIS CINEMA

This, another Brighton theatre that no longer exists, and which had an amazing history and nine different names over the years, stood in New Road, just a few doors down from the Theatre Royal; these views, taken in March 1962, show its last guise, as the Paris Cinema.

It had started life back in June or July 1863, as the Pavilion Wine and Spirit Music Rooms, but within months had become the Oxford Theatre of Varieties. Over the years it was home to such music hall greats as Dan Leno, George Robey, Little Titch, Marie Lloyd, Tom Costello and Albert Chevalier.

Rebuilding after a fire of March 1867, saw the first change of name, to the New Oxford. Over the next ten decades, it became the Empire, Coliseum, Court, Dolphin, Her Majesties and finally the Paris. The appeal of early cinema, saw the theatre showing films from 1909 and the building was bought by Gaumont British as one of its chain of 150 cinemas. Between 1947 and 1955 it was a theatre again, converting a final time to the Paris Cinema.

DEMOLITION OF THE PARIS CINEMA

Playwright JB Priestley described the Paris Cinema building as 'the loveliest theatre I have seen on the south coast'. The cinema's interior is seen again in March 1962, prior to demolition. The main view matches well with the one of the building coming down, taken in August 1964, from Bond Street, looking out from where the stage would have been. A campaign to save the theatre was supported by Sir Ralph Richardson, Sir Laurence Olivier and Charles Laughton, but came to nothing and an office building occupies the site today.

BRIGHTON FESTIVAL

The first Brighton Festival was held in April 1967, having as its symbol, the 'all-seeing eye', seen on the flags of the main view here, being set up in Old Steine. The other view shows a sculpture entitled 'Inter-67' about to be installed in Regency Square. This consisted of red, blue, yellow and black plastic globes arranged to form an 'environmental structure' ten feet tall. The most sought-after theatre ticket was probably for *Dance Of Death*, a play at the

Theatre Royal starring Sir Laurence Olivier and Geraldine McEwan.

  Growing from this first, mainly locally-based music and art festival, it continued to flourish and grow and now is generally considered second only to Edinburgh in size and scale.

In 1999, it promoted 532 events, brought some 195,000 people to Brighton over the three weeks it ran, with some events seen by millions on TV. 'It takes over the town,' said the *Sunday Times*, 'spilling into the streets, transforming churches into stages, artist's houses into galleries, and pubs into bandstands.'

PAINTING THE SEA

One amazing stunt of the first Brighton Festival was the ambitious plan to 'paint' a huge Union Jack on the surface of the sea between the piers. Well-known local fisherman Alan Hayes (still active today, running a fish stall opposite Brighton's Fishing Museum) is seen out in his launch, *Fair Chance*, with artist William Mitchell and assistants, who are putting the special dye onto the sea. The plan for a Union Jack had to be scrapped as the dyes were unavailable, so the idea was just to change the colour of the sea. 'The only effect,' wrote *The Argus*, 'was large splodges of fluorescent sickly green, which lasted more than an hour, discolouring the briny.'

Alan Hayes recalled: 'They arrived with a spray gun and two five-gallon drums of very concentrated crystals. Turning into the wind, the boat hit a wave and a cup of crystals flew into the air, covering the crew. Spray hit them and they all turned green.'

'I feel it has been an interesting interlude in the festival events,' William Mitchell said afterwards. He was also working on a sculpture, 'The Spirit of Brighton', to stand in the Churchill Square development, being built at this time.

MISS BRIGHTON

Black Rock bathing pool in July 1967, where a Miss Brighton contest is taking place. The winner was twenty-year-old Carol Ann Bull (right) a GPO telephonist of Denton Drive. Judges were folk-singers Nina and Frederick and Alderman George Lucraft. Miss Bull would be Miss Brighton again, the following year, plus Miss Brighton Carnival Queen. She would later marry Geoffrey Theobald, Mayor of Brighton in 1982, who in 2000 is Conservative Leader of the Opposition on Brighton and Hove Council. Their daughter, Natasha, was Carnival Queen in 1984. Black Rock pool closed in 1978 and demolished in 1984. The last council-organised Miss Brighton event would come a few years after this, then be held by various firms and clubs, including the Pink Coconut, now the Paradox.

CONCOURS D'ELEGANCE
AUTOMOBILE MEETING

Another 'beauty' contest, involving cars as well as the fair sex, is seen taking place in

June 1968 on Madeira Drive. This was a Concours d'Elegance Automobile meeting (elegant gathering of cars), staged by the Brighton and Hove Motor Club. Members could annually show off their vehicles and win prizes for various categories of car type.

On the left, Miss Carole Hardy poses on a Lotus Elan, winning for Peter King, its owner, the Mermaid Trophy for most attractive ensemble of car and passenger. The other picture is of Miss Jennifer Strachan, holding the Brighton Trophy, which she and Roger Marsden won for the motor trade section. The vehicle is a Ford Cortina 1600E.

The Concours d'Elegance began after World War Two and still takes place today. In June 2000 it was held in Stanmer Park.

THE BRIGHTON BELLE

More elegance, but this time in the form of the famous London to Brighton train, the Brighton Belle, seen approaching Patcham over the bridge at the bottom of Mill Road, during the 1960s.

The first Belle train was the Southern Belle, introduced at a cost of £40,000 in 1908 and described as 'the most luxurious train in the world'. From June 1934, three electric Brighton Belles operated, with five coaches each, allowing three services in each direction daily. The coaches had names such as Doris, Gwen and Hazel, and the interiors were again sumptuous. They were withdrawn from service during World War Two, but reinstated from October 1946. By the 1970s, the large number of catering staff employed proved to be uneconomic and the coaches needed replacing. Despite many protests, the trains were completely withdrawn in April 1972.

Today, the Railway Bell pub, near Brighton Station, still has the Brighton Belle pictured on its sign.

FIRE AT THE BEDFORD HOTEL

April 1964; the original Bedford Hotel, near the West Pier, was on fire. Hundreds of Easter-week visitors packed the seafront to watch. Two people died in the blaze. Although only the roof and upper storeys were destroyed, the whole building was subsequently demolished. Proposals to replace the hotel with a larger, modern building, had gone before the council only weeks before. Lewis Cohen had stated: 'This is a hotel which is completely out of date. The people who are proposing to rebuild the Bedford are doing a marvellous job of work for Brighton.'

The hotel was designed by Thomas Cooper and opened in October 1829. Charles Dickens wrote much of *Dombey and Son* while staying there.

The new 'state-of-the-art' hotel opened in September 1967. It has changed name several times in recent years; at present it's the Hilton Brighton West Pier.

TOWN HALL PROPOSAL

Another town hall plan, this one dating from 1965. The site is the same as before and again would involve demolishing the old 1830-31 Town Hall. The aerial view, of the same date, shows the site the new buildings would occupy.

The old Town Hall, seafront offices (previously the hotels seen on page 60) and the 1901 market building, which stood half demolished at this time and in use as a car park, would all be removed under the scheme.

DOLPHINARIUM

The Prince's Hall at Brighton Aquarium (smaller view) served mainly as a ballroom following the war, then, for a while, became The Flamingo Rooms night club. In 1961 it was converted into a museum for vintage motor vehicles, but the popularity of two dolphins at the Aquarium in 1968 led to the museum being transformed into a pool for dolphin shows. This is seen under construction in March 1969. It opened at Easter that year with seating for 1,000 spectators. In time though, animal welfare groups, campaigning against dolphin shows, pressurised the council into closing the pool and the last performances were in December 1990. The two remaining dolphins, Missie and Silver, were taken to the Caribbean for rehabilitation in March the following year. The Aquarium was subsequently remodelled as a SeaLife centre, at a cost of £1$\frac{1}{2}$ million, opening at Easter 1991, with the terraces above being largely rebuilt and modernised in 1999-2000.

SKYDECK TOWER

Brighton people were amazed in March 1964, when, out of the blue, the massive tower seen here, to stand on the seafront between the piers, was given serious consideration by the town's planning committee. Costing £1 million, it was to be known as The Skydeck.

'Gleaming like a silver rocket by day,' stated the *Brighton Herald*, 'aglow from the restaurant decking at night, and outrageously modern, it will attract thousands just for the chance to see the unrivalled view from the observation decking 600ft over the sea.'

The tower was to be 1,000ft high, built at the end of a 300ft pier. There would be three decks to the pier, for bars, a restaurant and a marine-type attraction where 'larger fish, such as dolphins and porpoises could be watched'. Three lifts, travelling at 700ft a minute, would carry 1,500 people an hour to the observation deck.

The proposers stated: 'The Eiffel Tower in Paris is seventy-five years old, yet last year it had a record number of visitors. In New York, the observation platforms at the top of such buildings as the Empire State are a major tourist attraction. We have studied towers all over the world and they fascinate people.'

This startling original proposal was another that obviously came to nothing, probably because it was just too extreme a structure for the town. During 1999-2000 however, Portsmouth City Council debated whether a massive tower, of similar proportions, should stand near the city's harbour entrance.

WEST STREET REDEVELOPMENT PROPOSAL

More plans that didn't materialise – not in the form seen here anyway.

This is one of many, many designs for what would become the Churchill Square and seafront development, following clearance of property seen on the map, back on page 78 .

One interesting feature is that the development doesn't encroach as far up as Western Road; shops here seem to have been left intact. But it's another case of nothing happening, yet always of course fascinating to see 'what might have been'.

THE GOOD INTENT
AND MILTON PLACE

Two photographs of sites that would be swallowed up for Churchill Square and its car park site, and of which no trace now exists. The Good Intent pub, below, stood in Upper Russell Street, opposite the top of Russell Street, and can be seen on page 78 , near the top of the picture, when both streets flourished and were part of a long-established community of fishing families. This view dates from December 1964.

  A year or so earlier, Milton Place, right, was photographed looking west, when the street was a jumble of old garages

and workshops. At the end (it was a cul-de-sac) stood what once was a large house, quite unlike others in the area, fronted with pebbles from the beach. This was Milton House, possibly an 1820s building. On the 1930 map, Milton Place is un-named, but is situated below Grenville Place, between Upper Russell Street and Clarence Street.

CANNON STREET CAR PARK

A view taken looking down from the Metropole Hotel, during the summer of 1965. The main building under construction, in the foreground, is what was then referred to as the Cannon Street

car park, as it covered the site of Cannon Street seen earlier in the 1950s. The car park would be rushed through, to be ready for the huge Toy Fair exhibition of 1966, then an annual event in Brighton, open only to traders.

In the middle distance, on the right, is the Cannon Street brewery, which would be demolished in 1969.

Between the brewery and St Paul's Church, is St Paul's School, the entrance to which was in Little Russell Street, demolished as part of the same site.

In between buildings left of centre, the cream frontage of the Academy Cinema can just be seen. This operated from 1911 to 1973.

To the right, cars are seen on the site that would become Churchill Square.

GRENVILLE PLACE

This is another street that would disappear for the Churchill Square development. It was one of the first streets to be built in the area, even before Western Road to the north of it existed.

Again, the map of 1930 (page 78) shows its location. The earliest record of Grenville Place is in 1803, when a weather report states that houses under construction in the street were damaged by storms. It seems to have been completely built up by the 1820s.

The southern side, which contained some really delightful cobble-faced houses with bow windows, came down first, in 1963, but the northern side survived

until 1967. 'It was one of those attractive small streets that have helped to give Brighton so much character,' wrote Antony Dale, in 1976. The picture here also shows parking meters, established in Brighton from March 1963. The cost was 6d an hour. They were removed in favour of the present voucher system, early in 1991.

DEMOLITION OF SHOPS IN WESTERN ROAD

With Churchill Square largely completed, final clearance work came with the removal of these shops in Western Road.

The main view shows them in November 1961, intact, the other view as they were coming down six years later.

The turning to Upper Russell Street can be seen next to Dorothy Norman's clothing store on the left. A tiny part of this street still exists today opposite the two pubs at the top of Cranbourne Street.

THE OPENING OF CHURCHILL SQUARE

The main picture shows Churchill Square in April 1968, six months before its official opening. Virtually everything seen earlier has gone, although a small part of Artillery Street can still be made out, on the extreme right, just below centre. The crane in the foreground is being used to construct the eighteen-storey Chartwell Court flats, completed in 1971.

Beyond the maze of buildings, the dark, curved roof of the Regent Dance Hall, in Queen's Road, can be made out. In the far distance, at the top of the picture, are the high-rise flats of the old Richmond Street area, now dominating this part of eastern Brighton.

The smaller view is of the spiral-shaped ground plaque, unveiled when Churchill Square was officially inaugurated, in October 1968.

UNIVERSITY OF SUSSEX

Another huge building project of the 1960s was Sussex University, established on the outskirts of the town, near Falmer village. There had been plans to establish a university in 1911, with £3,000 in funds available, but World War One saw the idea abandoned. Astute Herbert Carden included a university in his ideas for the City Beautiful in the 1930s. But it wasn't until June 1958 that the idea finally took off, and

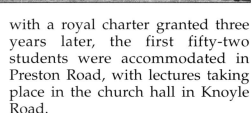

with a royal charter granted three years later, the first fifty-two students were accommodated in Preston Road, with lectures taking place in the church hall in Knoyle Road.

Meanwhile, work had started on the University complex, designed by Sir Basil Spence. The first building to open, in October 1962, was Falmer House, left, the student administrative and recreational building. The Gardner Arts Centre, above, was financed by the Gulbenkian Foundation and named after its director, Dr Lytton Gardner. It opened in late 1969, with a performance of *Comrade Jacob* by John McGrath.

STUDENT DEMOS

A large group of Young Socialist students from Sussex University march along King's Road to protest at the way the Labour Party, holding its 64th conference at the Top Rank building that month, was handling several key issues at this time. These included unemployment, particularly in the car industry and the wage and price freeze the Wilson government was about to impose.

Many were protesting about the Vietnam War too. The days of youngsters being seen and not heard were definitely over!

MODS ON DALTON'S BEACH

Another photograph where youth predominates. This is the scene on Dalton's Beach, the one immediately east of the Palace Pier, which appears to be taken over by teenagers. The date is the Bank Holiday of April 1964; not long after this picture was taken, the infamous clash between Mods and Rockers took place on the Aquarium terraces, detailed in Volume I.

This huge group all seem to be Mods, judging from their dress, and as all seems calm and relaxed, the picture was probably taken shortly before the Rockers arrived.

MODS AND SCOOTERS

The preoccupations of Mod culture never really died out, and in 2000, although there doesn't seem to be a youth group on which a name can be hung, the emphasis for most young people is still on wearing fashionable clothes, listening to pop music, partying and owning a vehicle of some kind, just as it had been for the Mods, forty years previously.

This picture, taken on Madeira Drive somewhere in the 1960s, shows a line -up of scooters, the bikes all self-respecting Mods just had to own. Judging from the sleeping bags rolled up behind the rear seats, many would be sleeping rough under the pier.

GROSS FACTORY

In the post-war period, industry in the central Brighton area dwindled away, leaving a huge number of old factories, brewery buildings and large workshops standing empty. Even Allen West, which in the 1960s employed something like 3,500 people, has only just about hung on and today has fewer than 100 workers.

A small industrial estate was established at Hollingbury from 1948. The unit seen in both views here, in August 1968, is Gross Cash Registers Ltd. The building dates from 1960. This firm was at its peak just before decimalisation in 1971, when changes to cash registers throughout the country generated huge business and three premises on the estate were occupied.

However, the firm failed shortly afterwards and all the buildings closed. Wade Engineering subsequently occupied the site of the one seen here. Today it is occupied by the Maclean Group.

In the 1970s the estate provided employment for more than 1,600 workers, nearly all in engineering or manufacturing jobs. Successive recessions reduced this considerably and by the 1990s several premises were empty and the estate began to look run down.

KEMP TOWN BREWERY

This view shows redundant industrial premises on the southern side of St George's Road in January 1970. These belonged to Kemp Town Brewery; brewing took place here until April 1964.

Charringtons, which took over the brewery in 1954, had moved to new premises at Newhaven. The old property came down in 1970 and was replaced by terraced housing.

Kemp Town Brewery was established in 1908 by Abbey and Sons, which previously had been Hallett and Abbey. William Hallett (inset) had been Mayor of Brighton in 1855 and had founded the Bristol Brewery about 1839. He also built a number of properties in Kemp Town, including St John the Baptist church.

QUEEN'S PARK – DERELICT SPA

A 'people's protest' took place in Queen's Park during April 1975. Residents in the area turned the grounds of the park's historic spa building into an allotment, protesting against plans to convert it into a casino and restaurant. They wanted it made into a nursery school and their campaign was eventually successful, the spa being partially restored and the school opening in 1977.

A street newspaper called *QueenSpark* grew out of the campaign and was sold from door to door. Out of this came the inspiration for the first book published by the group (in 1975), the robustly-written *Poverty – Hardship But Happiness*, by Albert Paul, about life in Brighton between 1903 and 1917. It was reprinted several times and a string of equally successful local books followed.

The spa building had opened in 1825, when the park was known just as Brighton Park, selling artificial spring waters to the town's wealthy visitors. King William IV patronised the building, along with his wife Queen Adelaide; the park was then named Queen's Park, in her honour.

CHURCH STREET — THE CENTRAL SCHOOL

Another building of the 1820s is seen here, but one that no longer exists. 'Perhaps the most shocking demolition that has taken place in Brighton,' was how historian Antony Dale described the removal of the Central Voluntary School building, which stood in Church Street, directly opposite the end of New Road. It was built for the Vicar of Brighton, HM Wagner, in 1829 and what made it particularly unique was that it was one of only two examples of Regency Gothic architecture in Brighton. The school closed in March 1967 and was cleared for road widening in 1971, when a postal strike made all communication about trying to save it impossible. 'Five years later,' Dale wrote, 'the road is un-widened and the gaping void is an obscene reminder of the criminal folly of this demolition.'

Twenty-four years later the site is still occupied by advertisement hoardings and awaits redevelopment as part of the adjoining Jubilee Street site, which has been derelict for over two decades.

The smaller view shows some of the school's 105 pupils at the main door, the day before it closed. They would transfer to a new school, in Centurian Road.

AMERICAN EXPRESS OFFICES

Brighton lost several significant buildings in the 1970s, but it also gained them. Here, the massive American Express building is seen under construction in July 1976, at a cost of £15 million. It took three years to complete – from May 1974, when the first ground was broken, to May 1977. Known as Amex House, it was the firm's largest building outside the US at this time, initially employing some 1,300 staff. At the opening ceremony, in September 1977, the Mayor, Councillor Mrs Hilary Somerville, described the eight-storey building as, 'a truly attractive combination of strength and elegance.'

It was soon nick-named, 'the wedding cake', because of its white-layered styling, and the building is now a landmark in the town, weathering remarkably little over the years.

THE GREAT OMANII

Before leaving the 1970s, in the mad and wonderful tradition of eccentric seaside entertainers at Brighton, we see The Great Omanii preparing to leap from the West Pier, in an escape stunt said to be replicating one performed by the great Houdini, when appearing at the Hippodrome, in Middle Street, back in the early 1900s. Actually he wasn't, because Houdini's escape was between the piers, where he was flung, bound and chained, into the sea from a paddle-steamer, but with crazy stunts at a premium in the 1970s, who cared?

The escape took place in August 1974. The press reported: 'Stuntman Ron Cunningham had the holiday crowds gasping. He stood on the West Pier at Brighton, Sussex, hooded and locked in chains. Then he jumped into the 15ft deep water. It was calculated that he would drown in 150 seconds, but Ron took only ninety seconds to free himself and bob triumphantly to the surface, where he was rescued by lifeguards.'

The Great Omanii was a Brighton grandfather, Ron Cunningham, who made the headlines from the 1960s onwards, by performing all kinds of amazing stunts, mainly on the West Pier, like jumping into the sea set ablaze with petrol, driving a speedboat under the pier blindfolded, or eating light bulbs. Ron's autobiography, *The Crowd Roars*, was published in 1999.

ROYAL WEDDING STREET PARTY

In Brigden Street (seen here), as everywhere else, street parties and celebrations were held in July 1981 to celebrate the wedding of Prince Charles, heir to the throne, and Lady Diana Spencer. Surprisingly, she was the first English woman to marry into the royal family for 300 years.

Electrical stores throughout the country sold an extra 35,000 video recorders to people wanting to record the wedding, and on the actual day, 22,000,000 watched the ceremony live on television.

LOUIS TUSSAUD'S WAXWORKS

From 1937 until 1980 there was a small waxworks on Brighton's seafront, operating from what used to be known as Clive House, but which now is part of the Royal Albion Hotel. The main photograph shows the building gutted, prior to the frontage coming down, in August 1981, when the premises were converted into a restaurant.

One of the first figures displayed was Jesse Matthews, a 1930s variety star. The last personality created was John Travolta, of *Saturday Night Fever* and *Grease* fame, two pop musicals of the 1970s.

The best figure was generally

considered to be Winston Churchill, which, on closure, went to the Tussauds display on Blackpool promenade.

The smaller view shows the Beatles figures, the legendary 1960s pop group, who would subsequently lose their suits and be displayed in their shiny Sgt Pepper uniforms during the late 1960s.

The restaurant on the site lasted a number of years, but the premises were absorbed into the Royal Albion Hotel in the summer of 1989.

" PHOTOGRAPH OF THE MODELS AT LOUIS TUSSAUD'S WAXWORKS "

THE BEATLES.

58 WEST STREET

In May and June 1987, this old house in West Street – for many years three small shops – was demolished, with few noticing it go, or caring when it did. It was on the eastern side of the street, between the Carpenter's Arms pub (since renamed) and Academy House, site of the old cinema. It was significant because, apart from number 72, further down, it was the only early nineteenth-century house left in the entire street. It was probably built around 1810, but the demolition went ahead on the grounds it had been altered so much over the years, it wasn't worth saving. The other view shows the offices that replaced it.

It is exactly this steady erosion of small, historic buildings that causes such concern among groups like the Regency and Brighton Societies, and other watchdog community groups in the town. Gradually, month by month, year-by-year, Brighton takes on the nondescript appearance of everywhere else and the uniqueness of even modest, small-scale buildings is lost.

DEMOLITION OF NORTH ROAD BATHS

In July 1972, *The Argus* reported that a committee of councillors looking at swimming facilities in Brighton considered North Road's baths to be 'unhygienic, inefficient, expensive and antiquated', and ought to be replaced by new £500,000 baths in redevelopment plans for the Jubilee Street area.

In the previous year 51,564 people used the pool – showing it was popular - but this was seen as a case of 'beggars can't be choosers', there being no other similar facility in central Brighton.

All this led to the closure of the baths, in November 1979, with demolition following two months later (the main picture).

Rapid building of a new, state-of-the-art pool, on a neighbouring site, to be known as the Prince Regent, took place during 1980-81. This is on the left of the smaller view, with the rear of the old North Road baths on the right.

The Prince Regent opened in April 1981, at a cost of £2.5 million.

SKINHEADS AT DUKE'S MOUND

Twenty years after the infamous Mods and Rockers disturbances in Brighton, a view of another youth group 'grounded' by police at Duke's Mound, Black Rock, after causing trouble in the town. These are skinheads, a working-class youth cult, which actually had its origins back in the late 1960s. The name obviously comes from their shaved heads; they dressed in a 'uniform' of white T-shirts, jeans, braces and 'bovver boots'. Skinheads became synonymous with racism, football hooliganism and right-wing extremism.

The smaller view shows a group being chased by police down Steine Lane towards East Street. Both views date from the Bank Holiday Monday of April 1984.

BUS TOUR BY BRIGHTON AND HOVE ALBION

A bus sweeps past the Palace Pier on a wet evening in May 1983, with members of Brighton and Hove Albion filling the top deck. They are touring the town following the 'finest hour' in the club's history - playing in the FA Cup Final against Manchester United. Initially they drew 2-2, but were defeated 0-4 in the replay. The final was watched by a crowd of 100,000 fans and some 600 million spectators on worldwide TV. The manager at this time (seemingly wrapped in plastic sheeting in the photograph), was Jimmy Melia.

This plaque commemorates the completion
of the one thousandth home
in the Whitehawk Redevelopment Area
at 14, Pett Close.
Unveiled by the Chair of Housing Committee
Councillor GILL HAYNES
27th September 1988

Director of Technical Services
MICHAEL KEARNS

Borough Housing Manager
MICHAEL J.ELBRO

REBUILDING THE WHITEHAWK ESTATE

Many of the houses of the original Whitehawk estate were poorly built and by the 1970s the place was very run down and out of date. It was decided to rebuild the estate, virtually from scratch, and a period of huge redevelopment began in 1975, which lasted well over a decade.

September 1988 saw the 1000th new home completed. In this picture, Jean Munday is welcomed to 14 Pett Close, by Councillor Gill Haynes, chairman of the housing committee.

DEMOLITION OF COUNCIL OFFICES

Another significant 1980s building project was building a new hotel on Brighton's seafront.

Behind it, forming a new square, would come - at last - a new civic centre for the council on precisely the site Herbert Carden planned one, back in the 1930s. The hotel would be called the Ramada Renaissance and would extend across the southern end of Market Street, bordering onto Little East Street. This meant the design would block off part of an extremely old Brighton street and the square would actually be a dead-end, with no view or way through to the seafront, when approached from the Old Town area beyond.

The main view here, of July 1983, shows the old council offices that would be demolished for the project. These were the hotels seen back in the 1920s photographs on page 60, taken over by the council after World War Two. The other picture shows their demolition in October 1984, viewed from the old Town Hall building.

BUILDING THE RAMADA HOTEL

A view taken from Market Street, looking south, in August 1986, showing work on the Ramada Hotel and new civic centre taking place. The southern end of Market Street has gone, but the old Town Hall of 1830 survives the redevelopment, standing strangely at odds with its modern counterpart opposite.

The hotel was built jointly by the firm of Speyhawk and Brighton Council, with the council having a 25% share in the hotel. It cost £25 million and opened in July 1987 with 204 bedrooms. The cheapest rate was £95 a night for a single room, without breakfast.

These prices didn't seem to deter customers and the

hotel was soon ordering fifty crates of champagne a week and had placed 1,800 rubber ducks in the bathrooms for guests to play with!

OPENING OF THE RAMADA HOTEL

The late Roy Castle led the official opening ceremony of the five-star Ramada Hotel, in September 1987. He was MC for a 24-hour marathon opening, which included hosting a fashion show of clothes from 1900 to 1980, a tour of local children's homes in an open-topped bus, a Mad Hatter's tea party and a masked ball attended by 250 people, including the Mayor, Councillor Raymond Blackwood.

The other view here shows the square of shops, with offices above, behind the square, in December 1988. The wall of the old Town Hall is on the right, with the rear entrance of the Ramada on the left.

THE LAST BRIGHTON FORGE

As the vast Ramada was unveiled on Brighton's seafront, a few streets away a small, but significant, industrial building was about to close, marking the end of another era in the town.

The main view here, of October 1991, shows the interior of Blaber's foundry in Portland Street, with Joe Ayling sweeping up. The firm had existed for eighty years and would be the very last Brighton foundry to close. A large office building, which has yet to be built, was announced for the site.

The foundry had made aluminium, brass and bronze castings for all manner of items, from door handles and lanterns to complex machinery parts. It made the brass fittings for restoration work at the Royal Pavilion, and for the Bluebell Railway's Pullman coaches.

Summer temperatures in the works would rise to as much as 110°F.

THE BRIGHTON BYPASS

The building of the bypass was the town's biggest road project of the century and takes this book to the period of the 1990s. Running from Shoreham to Stanmer, the eight-and-a-half-mile bypass was opposed by Brighton Council and 2,000 members of the Anti-Brighton Bypass Association, but it went ahead on the recommendation of the government. Opposition led to the largest public enquiry ever

for a non-motorway scheme, lasting ninety-seven days; this and other hold-ups delayed the bypass for seven years.

Work finally began in July 1989, at an estimate of £50 million. The first stage was the Patcham interchange, and the length of bypass eastwards up to Dyke Road. The old roundabout at the top of King George V Avenue, Hove, is seen in the main view being massively enlarged in September 1990. The other view, of September 1991, shows a huge swathe through Stanmer Wood taking the bypass to the Lewes Road. The Varley Hall student flats and part of Coldean are on the right, with Hollingbury, Old Boat Corner and the Downs in the distance. The Brighton bypass opened in sections, between 1991 and 1996.

VISIT OF PRINCESS DIANA

Nine years after her marriage to Prince Charles, Princess Diana is seen outside the Brighton Centre in July 1990, where she was attending an international congress concerned with family issues.

At this time she was still the most famous woman in the world. She would divorce Prince Charles in August 1996 and, as everyone knows, would die in a car crash in the Alma tunnel, Paris, in August 1997. Even three years on from the event, it's still hard to believe it actually happened.

CENTENARY OF THE LONDON TO BRIGHTON CAR RUN

November 1996 saw the historic centenary of the London to Brighton Veteran Car run – the 'Old Crocks' race. More than 600 cars started from the Metropole Hotel, Hyde Park, with twenty-five breaking down along the sixty-mile route. The winner was an 1898 Panhard Levassor, driven by Mike Timms, from Uckfield.

The original rally, called the Emancipation Run, was to celebrate the repeal in November 1896 of the infamous Locomotive Act of 1865, which decreed that any mechanically propelled road vehicle must be preceded by a man with a red flag, walking at two miles an hour in town, four in the country.

Those vehicles taking part today must have been built before 1905 to qualify; they also need a current MOT certificate.

The smaller view shows the very first London to Brighton run, of November 1896, which ended outside the Metropole Hotel, King's Road. This first run produced all kinds of ungentlemanly capers, including the driver who broke down, but got his vehicle to Brighton by putting it on the train! Of this first race, thirty hopefuls started, with only seventeen making the finish. As there were no garages in the town, the vehicles were stored overnight in stables at Waterloo Street, Hove, before heading for home.

MERGING OF BRIGHTON AND HOVE, AND CITY STATUS BID

In April 1997, the seemingly impossible happened; Brighton and Hove officially combined into one, single administrative authority. Ideas for such an amalgamation had been put forward many, many times in the past, but had been firmly resisted, particularly by Hove, which wanted to be independent from raffish Brighton and look after its own affairs.

In August 1999, an application was made to have the Queen grant the combined towns city status, to mark the new millennium. 'The place to Be' campaign started up, encouraging community, educational and business projects to aid the effort.

Thirty-nine towns applied and at the start of 2000 things looked very promising, with bookmaker William Hill announcing odds of four to one in favour of Brighton and Hove. Some punters were placing bets of £1,000 on the combined towns winning. Luton was second in the running, followed by Guildford, Reading and Milton Keynes.

However, by March 2000, Wolverhampton had become favourite, edging Brighton and Hove into second place. A Home Office circular stated that the weak link in Brighton and Hove's bid was a doubt over how closely the previously separate towns were now actually connected. Despite this, city status was awarded to Brighton and Hove in December 2000.

THE WEST PIER

An aerial view of the West Pier, taken in the summer of 1998, showing the amazingly dilapidated condition it was in at this time. It has been said the decline of the pier, starting in the 1950s, can almost be seen as mirroring the decline of Brighton in the post-war period.

Lack of revenue had led to lack of upkeep and the structure slowly rotted away, with the late 1960s owners, AVP Industries (a London-based furniture company), doing little to maintain the pier and invest in its future. Plans to restore the pier then came and went, sections of it had to be removed, parts collapsed, backers slipped away and the whole saga of the pier through the 1980s and early 1990s was a catalogue of high hopes, huge drive, but low realisations.

The real breakthrough was the £14 million lottery money awarded in 1998, but projected dates for the rebuilding proved over-optimistic – *The Argus*, in March that year, was reporting that the pier would be restored by the spring of 2001.

In 2000, the cost of rebuilding the pier, to deck level, is still put at £30 million. It won't stay at that of course, and unless work begins in a big way soon, the costs will surely escalate out of reach. The building of Brighton Marina forms a sobering comparison. The estimate for the Marina, with some fifty buildings and amenities on it, was £9 million in 1965. When the Marina opened in 1979, fourteen years later, without a single building or attraction on the site, the cost had been £41 million. How much will the West Pier be in three, five or ten years time? The answer is, simply, too much.

REBUILDING OF CHURCHILL SQUARE

The 1960s Churchill Square development dated rapidly, and by the 1990s had become very run down. Many shops were empty, some buildings were dilapidated and it was clear the place needed modernising and given a new 'feel' as well as look, to bring it in line with shopping malls in other towns.

This picture shows the £90 million 'look' the square was given, appearing from the air like a set from a science fiction film. It dates from summer 1998, prior to opening in September that year. Western Road is near the bottom of the picture, with the top of North Street on the left.

In December 1999, it was announced that the complex had won a top award from the British Council of Shopping Centres for the best-designed centre in the UK.

Russell Street, Upper Russell Street, Russell Place, Grenville Place, Cannon Street, Blucher and Milton Place were part of this site and their demolition, along with all the other streets and courtyards, wasn't just the loss of buildings; a whole community and way of life slowly died, just as in the Carlton Hill area during the 1930s.

SOLAR ECLIPSE

The Palace Pier began this second look at Brighton throughout the twentieth century, and ends it, seen here during the eclipse of the sun that took place on August 12, 1999. It happened at 11.20am, with the pier's illuminations coming on, as day turned eerily to night. Some 10,000 people gathered on the seafront to watch the event, many using special glasses sold to view the eclipse safely.

There was another kind of eclipse the following

year when, following the centenary of the Palace Pier in May 1999, its owners decided to change the name to just 'Brighton Pier' for 'geographical' reasons. The idea was met with huge derision by Brightonians. The Noble group was clearly worried that the impending restoration of the West Pier would steal the limelight and take interest and – eventually – customers away from their pier. Time will tell!

Photograph: Ray Ede

ABOUT THE AUTHOR

Chris Horlock lives at Shoreham, with his wife and two children, although he was born at White Street, Brighton, in 1953, and lived in the town for more than thirty years.

He went to Park Street Infants School (demolished in 1986), St Luke's Junior School (still there) and the Secondary Technical School, Hanover Terrace (demolished in 2000). In 1976 he obtained an honours degree in Education at the University of Sussex, after four years of teacher training. He first taught at Glebe Middle School, Southwick, then moved to Thomas a Becket Middle School, Worthing, where he works today.

As well as lecturing all over Sussex on aspects of Brighton's history, he has many other interests. He has always been able to draw and provides illustrations for books, magazines and greetings cards. He also has a passion for theatre and has co-written three musicals for children to perform: *Boy David, The Whale's Song* and *Cowboys and Indians*. His first adult play, *Magpie's Child*, will be premiered in Brighton in 2002 – during the Brighton Festival.

He has a further Brighton book planned: *Brighton Then And Now*, to be published in two volumes, where photographs of the past are presented alongside modern views, taken at exactly the same location.